S/n Lit.

Whisper Louise

Also by David Duff:

Biographies
ELIZABETH OF GLAMIS
ALBERT AND VICTORIA
HESSIAN TAPESTRY
MOTHER OF THE QUEEN
THE SHY PRINCESS
EDWARD OF KENT
PRINCESS LOUISE, DUCHESS OF ARGYLL
THE DUKE OF CAMBRIDGE (with E. M. Duff)

Travel
VICTORIA TRAVELS
VICTORIA IN THE HIGHLANDS

Novels
LOCH SPY
CASTLE FELL
TRAITORS' PASS

Essay
MAN OF GOD—The story of a Norfolk Parson

Whisper Louise

Edward VII and Mrs Cresswell

DAVID DUFF

FREDERICK MULLER LTD · LONDON

First published in Great Britain 1974 by
Frederick Muller Ltd., Victoria Works, Edgware Road,
London NW2 6LE

Copyright © David Duff 1974

ISBN 0 584 10336 0

Printed in Britain by Clarke, Doble & Brendon Ltd., Plymouth
and bound by Mansell Bookbinders Ltd, Witham, Essex

Contents

Illustrations

(between pages 96 and 97)

Preface

In the days of Queen Victoria there were many names which were taboo in the clubs and at the fashionable dinner tables, names which were spoken only in whispers. A slip from grace was seldom forgiven or forgotten, while an accident of birth could mean oblivion and lack of identity for an innocent person. A decision in court could damn for ever someone whose guilt was in doubt. Should Sir William Gordon-Cumming have been ostracised for the remainder of his life because he was accused of cheating at baccarat at Tranby Croft? Did Colonel Valentine Baker really try to rape the governess in the railway carriage between Midhurst and Esher? Was Lieutenant Carey guilty of cowardice when the Prince Imperial of France was killed in a skirmish with the Zulus? Did Lady Beresford deserve the rigorous social boycott to which she was subjected by the Prince of Wales?

Partisanship and feuding were a part of the life of imperial Britain and the ruthless discipline exercised by commanders, in the field and on the sea, was reflected in the social code. There was a surfeit of power in the hands of a few, and a degree of solipsism which, on occasions, bordered on the sadistic. There was a deficiency of mercy, and the finding of a scapegoat was a common means of hiding a mistake of others. The lack of popular communications media allowed many a wrong to pass unrighted.

Louise Cresswell was a victim of this prevailing bent. Through it she lost both her home and her way of life, and went into exile. She was a victim of a vendetta because she refused to sacrifice herself for the pleasures of the Prince of Wales, pleasures which he deemed to be a regal right. Because she put her case before the public, her name became taboo in royal circles. But she had many friends and they whispered of her doings—hence the title which I have chosen for this book.

In the flood of deific propaganda which greeted King Edward VII's approach to the Throne, Louise was damned as a hostile witness seeking revenge for supposed grievances. In latter-day biographies there has been little understanding of her problems and of her sadness, and it was left to H.R.H. the Duke of Windsor to say a few kind words on her behalf. It is because it would appear that she was wronged and hardly done by that I have retold her tale. Beyond doubt, she was courageous and modern-thinking, loving and intelligent. She was also an individual and a fighter. If she had not been, she would have become just a nonentity on a royal estate, with only the wan smile of Albert Edward to give her comfort.

I am indebted to Lady Harrod, a member of the Cresswell family and co-author with the Rev. C. L. S. Linnell of *Norfolk— A Shell Guide*, for providing me with information on, and photographs of, Gerard and Louise Cresswell; to Mrs Evelyn Noel for allowing me to read the diary of Mrs Francis Cresswell (Rachel Fry); to Mr Bryan Hall for permission to reproduce the portrait of the sons of Mr and Mrs Francis Cresswell; and to Mr Bernard Campbell for providing me with a photograph of Sedgeford Hall. My particular thanks go to Mr Edgar Reeks of King's Lynn for his patient research among local records. I am grateful, once again, to my wife and Mrs Fenella Baines for advice and assistance with the manuscript, and to Mrs J. M. Rochester for typing it.

DAVID DUFF

Weybread, December 1972–April 1974.

1

Introductory

The eldest son of Queen Victoria and Prince Albert was born on 9th November 1841. At the age of four weeks he was created "the Most High, Most Puissant and Most Illustrious" Prince of Wales. He was christened Albert Edward at St George's Chapel, Windsor, on the 20th of January 1842. The Duke of Wellington carried the Sword of State and King Frederick William of Prussia was a godparent.

In the family the boy was known as "Bertie". In later life his sobriquet was "Tum-Tum",[1] which at least savoured more of humanity than the labels of "Eliza" and "Joseph" tied to his parents.[2] The Prince laid no stress on his first name, signing himself "Albert Edward" or merely "A.E." When he came to the Throne he disposed of "Albert" and became plain King Edward VII. This was contrary to the wishes of his mother, but he said that his father had been universally known as "the Good" and he desired that his name should stand alone. And so it has.[3]

Of all the places upon which Albert Edward, Prince of Wales, made impact, from New York to Allahabad, Montreal to Luxor, Moscow to Paris, Biarritz, Carlsbad and Copenhagen, none felt his presence more deeply than the peaceful county of Norfolk, England. His stately home of Sandringham is a monument to him and to his lovely Danish wife. His fifty years there brought a revolution in the way of life. The tales about him are legion.

There are still those in East Anglia who can recall, from their childhood days, the fierce discussions which took place among their elders on the subject of the long and bitter fight which waged between the Prince and his attractive lady tenant-farmer. Although between the Crimean and the Boer Wars the "goings-on" and actions of Albert Edward occupied a large part of all conversation in Norfolk, the affair of Louise Cresswell was a case apart. Here he meddled with a matter close to the hearts of the people among whom he had chosen to dwell—the manner of the tilling of the land and the living of those who worked upon it.

For forty years the Prince provided a spring of chatter for the dinner parties in the mansions and the farmers' weekly lunches, for the tea parties of the ladies and the gossips of the nursery governesses, for the bars of the public houses and the clubs of Lynn and Norwich. Yet the happenings which were discussed were remote and detached from Norfolk—the Mordaunt divorce affair, the feuds with Lord Randolph Churchill and Lord Charles Beresford, liaisons with ladies in Paris and Vienna, the baccarat scandal at Tranby Croft. But Louise was a home problem. She was the tenant of Appleton Farm, part of the Sandringham estate.

When the Prince Consort, in a well meaning attempt to save his heir from the fate of social and moral disaster for which he was apparently heading, arranged that he should marry Princess Alexandra of Denmark and set up a domestic establishment in the heart of Norfolk, he created a "oneness" for the young Prince. "Oneness" can be interpreted as being the all-enveloping power of one person. Queen Victoria's "oneness" accompanied her throughout her Kingdom and most of Europe. To the amazement of Lord Salisbury, she even achieved it in Berlin in 1888.[4] The "oneness" of Bertie, when Prince of Wales, applied only completely at Sandringham. There he was omnipotent. He even interfered with the trappings of the Almighty. In Norfolk he could successfully curtail the length of the vicar's sermon to ten minutes. When he tried the same trick at Balmoral Dr Norman Macleod treated him to forty-seven full minutes, giving his opinion that neither the Prince nor any of his party had anything better to do than listen.[5]

Sandringham cost £220,000 and £60,000 was allowed for rebuilding and improvements.[6] This money came from the sum which the Prince Consort had accumulated for his son from the increased revenues of the Duchy of Cornwall. The expenditures suited the people of Norfolk well, and the thought that it was merely being transferred from the people of one part of the country to those of another, as a result of increased rentals, did not occur to them.

Sandringham reaped a golden harvest through the fifty years of the residence of its first royal squire. Model cottages were built for the workers, new schools appeared, lovely homes were provided for the higher grades among the staff, churches were restored, kennels, dairies, teahouses and farm buildings enriched the whole. Jobs were created—for gardeners, grooms, keepers, inside staff. There was constant occupation for those in the building trade. Here was an oasis of peace and security, while not far away brother families were lucky to get a piece of fat pork once a week and men were sent to Norwich jail for trapping a rabbit.

To enjoy this peace and security it was necessary to comply strictly with one rule. The wishes and requirements of H.R.H. the Prince of Wales were overriding. Those who wished to be rewarded with the good life were expected to bend the knee. Louise Cresswell was not that kind of girl.

In the main the trouble between her and her royal landlord was financial. In part it was a struggle against change—she wishing to retain the established way of life, while he was a firm believer in the old order yielding place to the new, a view which was to change when, as elderly King, he was forever moaning about the inroads of democracy.

Louise was a widow with a young son to support. Farming was hard work and provided but a scant income once the boom days of high prices caused by the Crimean War were over. If she was to survive it was essential that her men be allowed to work undisturbed and that game be kept within limits. Her idea of shooting was that two or three men should go out with a keeper and dogs and fire for sport and the pot. The Prince's notion, imported from Germany, was very different. He was a *battue* man. His ultimate aim was that the bags on his estate should be bigger than those on any other. He wished, at any cost, that his guests should be impressed and happy. He gilded the scene with magnificence—extravagant lunches in marquees, new painted game-carts, keepers in uniforms resembling those of German soldiers, an army of beaters in smocks and chimney hats.[7] The covers were designed so that the birds did not fly too high, while the hares were so multitudinous and tame that they did not realise what was going on until it was too late.

Despite her resistance to change, Louise was a modern thinking woman. By running a large farm single-handed over a century ago, she could be classified as a pioneer of "women's lib". But she could not balance her books if farming had to play second fiddle to the *battue*, when two days a week all work had to stop and her staff become beaters, when the woods and the covers were so full of game that crops were ruined by their feeding. She fought the royal juggernaut with all of her courage, of her strength and her skill, but in the end she was crushed beneath its wheels. She was

a victim of a revolution which changed not only the way of life
of Norfolk, but the social life of the country. She was sold up—her
treasures and her furniture, her animals and her implements—
and driven from the estate. Blinded with grief, she went to
America and there, travelling round the prairie farms, her strength
came back to her. She decided on a final round, and this she won.
She was already the author* of one book, and now she wrote a
second. In it she told of her years at Sandringham and her struggle
with H.R.H. the Prince of Wales. Word of this attack reached
Sandringham and counter steps were taken. On publication the
agent was ordered to buy up every copy that he could lay his
hands upon.[8] Thus this little book, 248 pages long, has today become a collector's piece.

Yet the relationship between Prince and widow was far from
being one of permanent thunder and frost. Very often, in the
eighteen years that they knew one another and were neighbours,
the sun shone and there were warm evenings of happy memory.
At times courtesy, compliment and sympathy flowed from this
unpredictable and changeable man. Not until the bitter end did
Louise become proof against his charm, a charm which, in fact,
few could resist. His sense of fun, his energy in enjoyment, his
gift of making everyone feel at ease regardless of their rank, drew
her towards him. It has been dubbed a "love-hate" relationship.
Perhaps, under differing circumstances, her feelings for him could
have sparked into love.

Louise's real hate was reserved for another man involved in
her troubles—the Prince's agent at Sandringham. This man she
loathed and despised—at one time she was tempted to take a
riding whip to him.

In fairness to the agent, he was in a most unenviable position.
Recruited from a local auctioneer's office, he was given the task
of running an estate on lines very different to those followed upon
others in Norfolk. The Prince was not an easy master. He did not
reason, as his father had loved to do. When anything went wrong,
he wanted to know immediately who was responsible. A head
fell, and that was that. But, this time in keeping with his father,
the Prince was generous when it came to handing out the country's
—and other people's—money, but very careful when parting with
his own. The result was that claims made by Mrs Cresswell for
damage and losses were not welcome, and it was the agent who
was caught between the squire and the tenant.

* *Norfolk, and the Squires, Clergy, Farmers and Labourers* (1874).

Another difficulty between the tenant and the agent was one of "class". "Class" was the yardstick of the countryside and the congregations on Sunday mornings were adjured to be content with the worldly rating allotted to them. "Class" determined the balls to which one was invited, the regiments and clubs one was able to join, and one's social circle. Louise was a "lady". When she went to the County balls at Sandringham, the footmen announced her loud and clear, "Mrs Cresswell", while the agent was busy behind the scenes ensuring that nothing went wrong with the arrangements. In the ordinary course of events the agent would have been the equal, or at best superior, to the tenant farmers for whom he cared. In this case, the balance was different and, as habitually happens in the relationship between the N.C.O. and the "gentleman ranker", the agent lay in wait for Louise, ever ready to lay the blame upon her.

With Louise out of the way, the fortunes of the agent flourished and he became an integral part of the estate which he had handled with such success. His grandchildren were blessed with regal ladies as godmothers and were the playmates of the grandchildren of the Prince of Wales—Edward VII as he became in 1901. Among the royal children was "David" of York, eldest son of Prince George who had married Princess May of Teck in 1893. "David" often visited Appleton House, by this time the home of his aunt Maud, who afterwards became Queen of Norway, and from the staff at Sandringham he heard many tales of the battle between his grandfather and Mrs Cresswell. He always remembered them. He had cause to remember the case of Louise Cresswell in 1936 when he became Edward VIII and was faced with the problem of cutting down on the cost of running Sandringham as a shooting estate.[9] In 1959, as Duke of Windsor, he recalled her case again when he was writing his book, *A Family Album*. He asked permission of the Queen to visit the Library at Windsor so that he might read again the words of Louise Cresswell in *Eighteen Years on Sandringham Estate*. In recounting how the agent had been instructed by Sir Dighton Probyn to buy up and destroy all copies of this book, as it gave considerable offence to his grandfather, he commented: "At Sandringham everything, including, I regret to say, the interest of the farmers, was subordinated to the shooting." After recording the spirited widow's continual guerilla conflict with her landlord over the harm done to her crops by his enormous operations for the rearing of game, he added: "But she could still write, despite her grievances, of my grandfather's 'extraordinary charm of manner and power of putting everyone at their ease, whether they might be driving a donkey cart or cleaning a grate, without a suggestion of patronage or difference of rank'."[10]

SOURCES

1 Anon. *Uncensored Recollections*, p. 317; Magnus: *King Edward Seventh*, p. 124
2 Kennedy: *"My dear Duchess"*, p. 11
3 Lee: *King Edward VII*, Vol. II, p. 5
4 *Letters of Queen Victoria*, 8th May 1888
5 Sanderson: *King Edward VII*, Vol. II, p. 94
6 Lee: *King Edward VII*, Vol. I, p. 143
7 Jones: *Sandringham—Past and Present*, p. 12
8 Windsor: *A Family Album*, p. 43
9 Windsor: *A King's Story*, p. 292
10 Windsor: *A Family Album*, p. 43

2

A Royal Enigma

Albert Edward, Prince of Wales, was an extraordinary character and a most unpredictable opponent. In the manner of Alice, when he was nice, he was very, very nice, and when he was bad, he was rather worse than horrid.

His mother early realised that there was something odd about him. She attributed this to the short interval in time between his birth and that of the Princess Royal.[1] In general, he caused her more trouble in his growing years than the remainder of her eight children added together. Looking at his "painfully small and narrow head, those immense features and total want of chin",[2] she called in a phrenologist to examine his cranium, but the contours revealed no secrets. His trouble was much deeper rooted, and could not be explained away by bumps on the head or the date of birth. Then Queen Victoria realised that he was a cruel caricature of herself,[3] and she did not relish the drawing which she saw.

The domestic tragedy of the Prince of Wales lay in the disappointment which he brought to his parents. Both were determined that, with them, a new era should begin and that the example of Victoria's "wicked uncles" should be wiped away. Albert was convinced that the future of the Throne in a changing world rested on the spotless example of the person who sat upon it. He told Baron Stockmar in 1846: "The exaltation of Royalty is possible only through the personal character of the Sovereign. When a person enjoys complete confidence, we desire for him more power and influence in the conduct of affairs."[4] Both believed that they could mould such a paragon.

They put their trust in education, although Lord Melbourne warned them of the danger of so doing.[5] Their careful planning came to nothing. Their hopes, their dreams were shattered, to be replaced by disillusionment and bitterness. When Bertie was eighteen his father described him as being possessed of an "indescribable laziness" and added: "I never met in my life such a thorough and cunning lazybones."[6] He bewailed the fact that such a boy "might be called upon at any moment to take over the reins of government in a country where the sun never sets."[7] His mother joined in the sad chorus: "Oh dear, what would happen if I were to die next winter! One trembles to think of it. It is too awful a contemplation!"[8]

After a tour of America and Canada, on which he proved immensely popular and was received with acclamation, Bertie's stock rose. But thereafter the future became even more awful for the parents to imagine. Their heir evinced a penchant for tobacco and the company of fast young men. There followed his sexual baptism in the bed of Nellie Clifden, an actress, who thereafter bragged about the experience. It was too much for the Prince Consort. He was overworking and worried about the war in America and the potato famine in Ireland.[9] He was driven near to distraction by the exaggerated grief of his wife over the death of her mother, behaviour which caused European circles to speculate upon her sanity. His cousins in Portugal were dying of typhoid. The new burden crushed him. He feared that the Crown, which he had polished so assiduously, was now tarnished for ever, and that the engagement of his son to Princess Alexandra of Denmark would be quashed by Copenhagen. He saw other dangers, such as the contraction of veneral disease and the arrival of an illegitimate child. The nightmare haunted him, and he lost the will to live.

The Queen put the blame for his death squarely on the shoulders of Bertie, not even bothering to call him to his father's deathbed. Having ferreted out "all the disgusting details" of his ill-advised experiment, she told Princess Frederick William that she would never again be able to "look at him without a shudder".[10]

As the years passed she learned patience and came to love him, a contributory cause of the change being his near fatal illness of December 1871. But she put no trust in him and would not delegate her power. She said of him: "Poor Bertie—his is not a nature made to bear sorrow, or a life without amusement and excitement—he gets bitter and irritable."[11] So she kept the reins of power in her implacable hands and although, in her last years, she handed over certain duties to the Prince of Wales, she remained in sole control until she died at Osborne in January 1901. It was then that Henry James wrote: "We all feel motherless today. We are to have no more of little mysterious Victoria, but instead fat vulgar dreadful Edward."[12]

Albert Edward made a better King than he had a Prince of Wales. He matured late and it is clear from a study of his life that inherited weaknesses and a poor medical background were strong influences on both his character and behaviour, as indeed had been the case with his father and his great-grandfather, George III, in differing ways. He died, worn out, at sixty-eight, and signs of his lack of stamina showed in the two generations which followed him. When the last of his six children died, three of those of Victoria and Albert were still alive and active. A son died in infancy and his heir, Prince Albert Victor—a premature child who grew into a most strange young man—at twenty-eight. His three pigeon-chested daughters died in their sixties, while King George V, surviving a serious illness in 1928, just reached seventy.

When Queen Victoria said that Bertie was not of a nature to bear sorrow, the words "and strain" might well have been added. This inability was clear in his own children, and also in his grandchildren, despite the injection of the strong blood of Queen Mary. A clear example was the case of King George VI, who was under severe stress from the time of his accession and died at the early age of fifty-six. The Duke of Windsor, who achieved comparative longevity by reaching seventy-seven, was the longest lived of his paternal forebears for three hundred years. Yet despite being spared the strain of kingship and despite the infinite care of his wife, a serious illness in his sixties might, under differing circumstances, have carried him away. The same physical defect occurred in the family on a number of occasions.

The fault cannot be laid at the door of Queen Alexandra. Her mother was a rumbustious Hesse-Cassel and a number of this family became nonagenarians. Her father, King Christian of Denmark, was a fit and active soldier and in marked contrast with the weak and childless King whom he succeeded. Born in 1818 and a one-time suitor of Queen Victoria, Christian lived until 1906. At the time of Alexandra's engagement a scar upon her neck had given some concern in London, scrofula and consequently a tendency towards tuberculosis being suspected, but the explanation was given that it was the result of a neglected cold. It was as a result of this scar that Queen Alexandra wore "a dog collar" and set the fashion for them.[13] One inherited weakness came from her mother, that being otosclerosis, a type of deafness brought on by pregnancy and illness. The birth of her third child and an attack of rheumatic fever carried this burden to her, and she became increasingly deaf with the passing years.[14]

As for Queen Victoria, both her parents were robust personalities. Although her grandfather, George III, was deemed to be mad, this was later discovered to have been porphyria, from which her father, the Duke of Kent, was believed to have been a sufferer to a minor extent, a state which may well have been responsible for his eccentricities. That her immediate forebears were as strong as they proved to be was surprising, when one considers that George III's father was the weak Frederick Lewis, Prince of Wales —"Poor Fred" who died at forty-four—and his mother was Princess Augusta of Saxe-Gotha, who died at fifty-two, the blood of her House being tainted with many a disease. She attempted to marry her eldest son to a Princess of Gotha who, on inspection, was discovered to be a cripple and incapable of bearing healthy children, a pointer towards syphilis. Fortunately her plans were thwarted.

Queen Victoria's physical strength was phenomenal. She had little patience with illness—she considered that death was the only excuse for not taking one's place at the dinner table. Her own sufferings were limited to typhoid fever in 1835 and an abscess under her arm in 1871. Over-work, worry over the Boer War and over-eating caused her death in her eighty-second year. It was from this fount of strength that Bertie inherited his capacity for dancing into the small hours and his ceaseless perambulations around Europe and the stately homes.

There was surprisingly little in him of his father, but a great deal of his licentious uncle, Ernest, Duke of Saxe-Coburg and Gotha, who kept a clutch of women in his park at Coburg. Albert ate sparingly—Bertie was a glutton. Albert eschewed alcohol and tobacco—Bertie was an addict of both. Albert had no time for women—Bertie could not exist without them. Albert loved to reason—Bertie made his decisions on the spot. Albert loved to read and study—Bertie disliked books, except for novelettes obtainable from station bookstalls. Albert played cards for counters— Bertie for stakes. Albert was bored by racing—Bertie was thrilled by it. Albert disliked moving in Society—Bertie was Society's star. With such in-built differences between them, it was not surprising that Albert lost patience with his eldest son.

Yet it was through the father that the innate weaknesses reached the son. As a child Albert was a weakling, suffering from croup, bronchitis, frequent feverish colds accompanied by nightmares, a bilious stomach and constant tiredness. He was a middle-aged man plagued by rheumatism by the time that he was twenty-five, and by his early thirties he was tiring fast. Strain, physical and mental, hastened that decline. And strain of both kinds there was a-plenty in the 1850s; whether it was, wet through, accompanying Victoria on the long Highland expeditions which she loved, or sitting day long at his desk dealing with the problems of the Crimean War, India, France and America. Unlike men of the calibre of Lord Palmerston, he could not put aside from his mind the problems which surrounded him. In any event, he had to cope, night and day, with the tempestuous emotions of his wife.

Pursuing the trail of Bertie's weaknesses backward through time, the cause of them may be laid at the door of the family of his mother—Louise of Saxe-Gotha. Although the Coburgs were odd and tainted with disease, they were not weak. Louise's mother died a few days after the birth of her daughter—an only child. Louise's father was an eccentric hypochrondiac who would often pass the entire day in bed. He died, in 1822, before he was fifty. The childless brother who succeeded survived him by only three years.

The health of Duchess Louise was a constant source of worry. As a bride of eighteen she complained that she "was horribly sick and needed to spit all the time". The Court physician diagnosed the cause as irritated nerves from overtiredness—the same weakness as appeared in her son.[15] At twenty-two she complained of constant pains in her stomach. "I had an inflammation of the bowels, and as a result of this a haemorrhage. . . ."[16] Mention of feverish colds, sweating and toothache appear often in her letters. She had a further severe haemorrhage when she was thirty and died of uterine cancer five months later.

Such was the stock from which Victoria and Albert planned to build a paragon ruler of "a country where the sun never sets". In the event there were to be no paragons among their children or grandchildren, although the Queen's strong blood carried some of them through to the ninety mark.

The conditions surrounding the birth of the Prince of Wales may well have proved to have made a deeper effect upon his character than did his inheritance—certain it was that these conditions were more arduous than those that were to be the lot of his brothers and sisters.

In the first place, his mother endured a most difficult confinement, which had been imminent for some weeks.[17] Unaccustomed as she was to exaggerate in such matters, she confided to her diary that the pain was "very severe", adding that she did not know what she would have done if Albert had not been at her side throughout.[18] She was furious at "being caught" again so soon, and the experience led to her being prejudiced against babies. In after years she wrote to her eldest daughter: "Abstractedly, I have no tendre for them till they have become a little human; an ugly baby is a very nasty object—and the prettiest is frightful when undressed. . . ."[19] She added that Albert felt the same, adding: "After a certain age if they are nice (and not like Bertie . . .) he is very fond of playing with them."[20] It would therefore appear that poor Bertie began his journey under a handicap. When her first grandchild was born, Queen Victoria prayed that "he won't be like the ugliest and least pleasing of the whole family"[21]—and she was referring to her heir.

In the second place, the Queen suffered from exaggerated pre- and post-natal depression. Although the post-natal may have influenced her adversely against her son, fortunately he was saved from ill effect as he was transported to a distant nursery at Windsor and saw little of his parents, partly owing to the heavy demand of State duties on their time and partly because the Queen's emphasis was on her daughter, an amusing and happy child. Bertie was fed by a wet-nurse, who received £1,000 for the service.[22]* But the pre-natal depression hit Bertie hard and was at the root of his failing when the time came for him to undertake the strain of education.

Victoria suffered this depression during her last seven months of pregnancy. She was a woman who was most jealous of "her own"—her possessions, her friends, her way of life. Since childhood her mainstay had been her governess, Baroness Lehzen. After her accession, the Prime Minister, Lord Melbourne, joined her intimate support group. Albert, in the beginning, was admitted in the rôle of plaything, a shadow who would blot her signature. She had no intention that he should intrude into politics[23] and was certain that he had no wish to—an indication of how little she knew of the Coburg ambitions.

It was in April 1841 that she began to feel the cold winds of change. It then became obvious that Melbourne's Government could not long survive, that his comforting arm would be taken from around her. In his place she would have to turn for advice to the chilly Sir Robert Peel, with whom she had already crossed swords. It was also clear that Albert and Baroness Lehzen were at loggerheads. On visits during the summer he arranged that the Baroness should be left behind to look after the children. Never before had Victoria slept without her governess being installed in the room next door.

* Unfortunately, in after years she murdered her own six children.

22

At the end of August Melbourne went out of office. The Queen had not realised that this would mean that her connection with him would be completely severed and that he would no longer be able to come round for a chat in the evenings, and this at a time when she needed him most. But that was the Coburg plan, and most ruthlessly was it carried out by Baron Stockmar. Victoria missed her old friend deeply and Albert had neither the maturity nor the wit to fill his place.

It was in September that Albert declared open war on Lehzen. With her long service and experience she considered that it was her duty and her right to be in constant attendance upon the pregnant Queen during the last, intimate months, and that the young husband should keep out of the way, contenting himself with hunting and lightening the public duties of the Queen. Albert had widely differing views, most unusual among fathers of the day. He wished to be in full control of his wife's health and welfare, adopting a rôle which she was to describe as that of "mother".[24] As the weeks passed, the rows between Albert and Lehzen became increasingly bitter. She openly defied him, telling him that he had not the power to oust her. He used propaganda and sarcasm to the full. He labelled her "the yellow lady", as she had suffered from jaundice, and accused her of "spitting venom like a she-dragon".[25] The struggle was but one more example of the ruthlessness of the Coburgs when dealing with women who crossed their path. Prince Leopold* had meted out the same treatment to Caroline Bauer, Duke Ernest I to Pauline Panam and, later, his wife,[26] and, in the years to come, Albert Edward, Prince of Wales, was to do so to Louise Cresswell.

The back-lash of the two feuds frayed the nerves of Queen Victoria and the autumn of 1841 proved one of the most unpleasant periods of her life. Her physical strength carried her through the birth, but the strife about her brought about a state of deep mental depression. It was little realised in those far off days that every disappointment that the mother underwent, every sadness, every shock and row, would be transposed to the child unborn, and that in due season the bruises would expose themselves.

A sad reflection upon Bertie's later troubles was that, when a young child, he was calm, sweet-tempered and easy to handle.[27] In the haven of the nursery he responded to love. He was spoiled by his nurse, Mrs Sly, and there were few troubles when he began

---

* King of the Belgians.

lessons under the care of the royal governess, Lady Lyttelton, and three mistresses. Although he did not develop, mentally or physically, as fast as had his elder sister, he was for the time being left in peace. Yet, behind the scenes, his father and Stockmar were preparing a programme aimed at producing a paragon. When the boy was seven and a half years old, the programme began. Prince Albert had agreed to "an educational plan of unparalleled rigour which made no allowance for human weakness".[28] Henry Birch, at the head of a team of tutors, pumped Geography, Calculating, German, French, Drawing, Music, Chemistry and Social Economy into the boy for five hours of the day for six days in the week. The change in Bertie was immediate. He rebelled, becoming impertinent and disobedient. Educational progress was slow and the parents blamed the tutor. Yet here came a strange reaction in the pupil. Despite the chastisement administered to him, he developed a *Schwärm* for Birch, "even as his father had had in days of early boyhood for his tutor Herr Florschütz."[29] Albert discovered that affectionate notes were passing from boy to master and, recognising the signs of a "disordered fancy", quickly replaced Birch by Frederick W. Gibbs.

Bertie hated Gibbs and the five years which he spent under him. The hours of study were extended to six, and sometimes seven, per day, and there were no holidays except family birthdays and feast days. Even at Balmoral he was kept at his desk while his parents and the younger children were picnicking in the hills. In the evenings there were periods of drill and gymnastics, under the eagle eye of an army sergeant, a precaution against sex rearing its ugly head. This treatment produced a tragic state of mind varying between total incapacity and maniacal rage. Warnings went to Prince Albert, the Queen and Stockmar, but were not heeded. Dr Becker, the librarian who taught German, put the case clearly in a long and outspoken document. He reported that, often after a period of study as short as five minutes, the boy showed clear signs of exhaustion and one might as well have tried to instruct someone who was fast asleep. If severity were used, he would seize any object handy and fling it through the window. At times he would rush into a corner, stamp his feet and scream.[30] Even his mother, ignorant as she was of psychology, learned the signs which pointed to the oncoming of such fits. She noted that, a day or so before, Bertie would hang his head and look aimlessly at his feet.[31]

Thus to the young Prince "work" became a dirty word, books an anathema. Pleasure, in all its forms, beckoned as sweet as forbidden fruit. His mind went into reverse, and idleness, tobacco, alcohol, sex, gambling and practical jokes evolved, with the years, into dreams for which his starved thoughts craved.

A lasting harm implanted upon him at this time came as an understandable reaction. This was the desire to hurt. It showed, among other directions, in his treatment of servants, much as a mentally backward person will vent his spleen on dumb animals. He tormented his valet, "pouring wax on his livery, throwing water on his linen, rapping him on the nose, tearing his ties and other *gentlenesses*".[32] He was also unpleasant to other boys, of whom he met too few. The failing was noted by all who came into contact with him. Stockmar, who was a qualified doctor, was consulted, and his reply was not encouraging to those at work laying the foundations for a King. The Baron replied that the madness of George III was reappearing in his great-grandson, adding that he had noted the same streak in the Queen's father, the Duke of Kent, and in her uncles, George IV and the Duke of Cumberland.[33] While this was correct as regards the sons of George III—George IV and the Duke of Kent also had been hardly treated and over-strained during their educational period and Cumberland was near to being a psychopathic case—Stockmar can hardly have been expected to lay the blame on a curriculum of his own devising.

This unpleasant streak was apparent in Albert Edward through-ont his entire period of sexual awareness, from the time of supervision by tutors to the time of the ebb of that awareness, when he was sixty and became King. It was succeeded by moods of black depression.[34]

It was apparent from his taste in practical jokes. He found obvious amusement in the discomfiture of both men and animals. He arranged for a trussed, live rabbit to be placed in the bed of Christopher Sykes.[35] A midshipman, at Sandringham for the first time and suitably impressed, bit into a mince pie to discover that it was full of mustard.[36] A donkey was hoisted up to a first floor window and, having been secured in the bed, was arrayed in night-wear.[37] The Prince of Wales laughing as he poured brandy over the head of poor Sykes, or burning his hand with a lighted cigar, was anything but a funny sight.[38] It has all been explained away by his disciples as part of the spirit of the times. Nevertheless, the streak of nastiness remains clear.

The Prince ruined many men who accepted his hand of friendship yet had not the background or finances to maintain such a part.

25

Poor George Dupplin! he was a strange personality—but lovable after all. His many failings sprang chiefly from the fact that his being taken up by the Prince of Wales led him into habits of extravagance that weakened his moral sense and led him to do things of which, but for this expensive Royal intimacy, he would never have been guilty. There were many similar cases. . . . Charles Buller, Joey Aylesford, Tom Pratt—*mais à quoi bon?* Their name is legion.

And when the sun fell on these men, the dark night followed swiftly.[39] Sykes was only saved from catastrophe by the exertion of strong feminine pressure.[40]

The worst streaks in Albert Edward showed when he was deliberately thwarted or defied. Then came a flash-back to his schoolroom days, when he had screamed and stamped and broken windows in a vain attempt to best his father and his tutor. As if in revenge for those days, as adult Prince of Wales the determination to lose no more was obvious. When White's club forbade him to smoke in the morning room, he stalked out and founded his own club—the Marlborough.[41] His notorious feuds included those with Lord Randolph Churchill and Lord Charles Beresford —although he chose the wrong man in Lord Charles, who rushed into Marlborough House with his fist raised, whereat the Heir sat on a sofa and said, "Don't strike me!"[42] Louise Cresswell had good cause to know of that evil temper. On occasion when the two were at loggerheads and came face to face on the Sandringham estate, she would glimpse the scowl on his face and a shiver would run through her. He reminded her of Henry VIII and she knew full well that, if she had lived in those early days, her head would have rolled.

There also appeared in the Prince of Wales a tendency to become involved in trouble, either for the excitement thus obtained or to show how expert he was at extricating himself. Unfortunately, it was his wife and mother who suffered more than he did. To say the least of it, it was imprudent of him to write letters to young Lady Mordaunt only four years after his marriage. Trifling as these letters may have been, the mere writing of them was sufficient for the Heir to the Throne to be called as witness in the divorce case brought by Sir Charles Mordaunt. The Queen wrote to the Lord Chancellor, Lord Hatherley:

> The fact of the Prince of Wales's intimate acquaintance with a young married woman being publicly proclaimed, will show an amount of imprudence which cannot but damage him in the eyes of the middle and lower classes. . . .[43]

Lord Hatherley stressed to the Prince the utmost importance of setting a strict example, his life being "as a city set upon a hill".[44] Mr Gladstone informed him that a return to the scandals of fifty years before might lead to the Monarchy being overthrown. The Queen also remonstrated, and her son replied: "I cannot sufficiently thank you for the dear kind words which you have written to me . . . I shall remember all the kind advice you have given me, and hope to profit by it."[45] In the event there was no sign in after years that he had heeded it at all. Even the fact that he was hissed at at the theatre and at Ascot did not make him change his ways.

His uninhibited attention to pretty women was an open invitation to criticism. After visits to Russia and France in 1867, Europe rang with tales of his romances. Princess Alice, the sister who understood him best, remonstrated with him, but he just smiled.[46] When he suggested to Mrs Wheeler, a Roman Catholic, that they should drive out together and that he would pick her up at her house in his private brougham, she declined on the grounds of possible adverse publicity. He told her not to mind what people said—they said all kinds of things about him but he did not care. "Perhaps not, Sir," was her reply: "But so far they say nothing about me, and I don't mean that they should."[47]

It was over the baccarat scandal at Tranby Croft in 1890 that the Prince demonstrated his apparent inability to avoid trouble. He made error after error. In the first place, he should not have suggested that baccarat be played. He knew his host, Mr Arthur Wilson, a wealthy shipowner from Hull, only slightly, and was only staying at Tranby Croft because his customary host for the Doncaster races, Christopher Sykes, was in no financial state to entertain him. In any case Mr Wilson did not possess a suitable table on which to play, and he disapproved of the young playing baccarat—the son of the house was twenty-two.

The man accused of cheating was Sir William Gordon-Cumming. He had been invited by the Prince, who called him "Bill". For some years past Sir William had been widely suspected of sharp practice. Having been seen so doing, certain of the guests condemned him as guilty and submitted the matter to the Prince of Wales. Instead of the Prince standing by his friend and avoiding scandal by leaving the house next morning, he participated in the ridiculous melodrama of forcing Sir William to give a written promise that he would never touch a card again, while, for their part, the guests in the know swore that they would never divulge what had happened. This childish bond of secrecy was broken within weeks. It was a feminine leak. Mrs Wilson's quick rise up the social ladder had made her many enemies, and the current girl-friend of the Prince was Lady Brooke, known as "the Babbling Brooke".

Sir William decided that he must go to court to clear himself. The Prince, now thoroughly frightened, tried to prevent this by putting indirect pressure on the War Office. But in the end he had to appear before the Lord Chief Justice.

The case was a *cause célèbre*, the talking point of the London season of 1891. When Sir William was pronounced guilty, the crowds in court hissed and the jury had to take refuge in a nearby inn.[48] The man who caught the backlash of the scandal was the Prince of Wales. For many years the Church and the solid institutions had been waiting the chance to expose his gay life, the round of racecourses and casinos, the lavish entertaining and the ever changing mistresses. Now it was revealed that the Heir to the Throne travelled round with his own set of "chips" given to him by a Jew and was prepared to play with young men half his age; that he was ready to twist the laws to suit his own ends; and that he had let down a friend whom he had long known as "Bill".

Now "Bill' was condemned to social ostracism and referred to by the Prince as "a damned blackguard". The Prince's efforts to extricate himself from this major scandal were masterly. Having summoned the Archbishop of Canterbury to Marlborough House, "he strongly affirmed that he was no gambler, that gambling, as he understood the word, was hateful to him, but that playing cards for small sums was no such thing". "They say that I carry about counters as a Turk carries his prayer-carpet, but the reason why I carry counters is to check high play."[49]

The counters ranged in value up to ten pounds. In two days play at Tranby Croft Sir William had won £225, mostly from the Prince, who held the bank.[50] From the study of the case there emerges one obvious point—the importance which the Prince attached to money. This was a root cause of his troubles with Louise Cresswell on farming matters. If he had paid out to her her rights, which was as pin-money compared to the sums that he won and lost at cards, he would have saved himself the experience of being denounced from the floor of the House of Commons.

His outlook on financial matters reminded Louise of the story about George IV. When Prince of Wales, he ordered goods from a Frenchman for the decoration of Carlton House. After a long interval during which he received nothing, the Frenchman pressed for payment. The Prince arranged that he be smuggled to Paris, where the Revolutionaries guillotined him. Equally averse to paying out, when Albert Edward was, at long last, asked to settle a fifty pound gambling debt, he replied, "Certainly. Twenty-five, wasn't it?", and quickly wrote out a cheque for that amount.

There were other ways in which the Prince defied public opinion, among them the patronisation of certain blood sports which were spurned by the mass of the people. The shooting of pigeons released from traps was one of these. A satirist wrote:

> A timid pigeon fastened in a trap
> At which, when loosened, they might stand and shoot
> Was sport well suited for strong men....[51]

Such indulgence is hard to understand as the Prince knew only too well that his wife loathed this so-called sport and was doing her best to bring it to an end, a result which she finally achieved. Cock-fighting was hardly to be recommended as a pastime for the heir to the Throne.[52] In March 1868 he was out with the Royal Buckhounds when a carted deer was chased through the streets from Harrow to Paddington station, where it was killed. The presence of the Prince brought an outcry from the press.[53]

The complete lack of sympathy for the hunted animal came from his Coburg ancestry. The ultimate in entertainment in the German Duchy was to shoot deer trapped in a corral. From the safety of a raised platform the men blazed away at the frenzied animals, while bands played and the ladies applauded.[54] The Prince Consort never accepted English, or Scottish, ideas on sport, this being one of the main reasons for his unpopularity with the land-owners. Fortunately Queen Alexandra's great love of animals was passed on to later generations of the Royal Family. Each winter's morning it was Alexandra's habit to thrown corn to the pheasants which awaited her coming on the lawn. When she noted that one of her pets was missing, a victim of the battue, there were moody silences throughout the day. There were other reasons for such silences, the main one being sex.

She came from a family which believed strongly in the ties of family life and placed the bond of children and relationship above the physical-emotional side of sex. She was not above pillow fights and apple-pie beds in the darkened corridors, but enjoyment was restricted to jokes. Marriage was for keeps. Her husband was of a very differing make-up. While his mother was highly sexed, his father, completely disinterested outside the marital bed, played the rôle of consenting mate, somewhat surprisingly when the

29

adventures of Dukes Ernest I and II of Coburg are considered. The result of the mixture was an unbalanced penchant for women's company.

Since the days of the Georges the members of the Royal Family have, in the main, been divided into one of two categories—the extrovert and the lymphatic. The former have fallen quickly, violently, even blindly, in love, the attainment of their goal being all devouring. The latter have approached love sedately through the door of marriage and allowed the bond to grow stronger with the years. Contrasting examples are George IV and Adolphus, Duke of Cambridge; Princess Louise and Princess Beatrice; Albert Victor, Duke of Clarence, and George V. Princess Louise threatened to enter a convent if her matrimonial plans were thwarted, while her namesake of Wales warned that, if anyone crossed her, she would put her head into one of those new-fangled gas ovens.[55] There are other examples of this categorisation closer to hand.

Albert Edward was the most extrovert of the extrovert. He carried the label which Christopher Hibbert has tied to both George IV and the Duke of Windsor—"too much of a lady's man to be the man of any lady".[56] Change and new experience were an essential to him. His enemy was boredom. He used the royal status as an aphrodisiac and took whom he desired. By so doing he destroyed much of the mantle of sanctity but recently cloaked around the institution by his parents. Yet in this failing, as distinct from others such as gambling, his widowed mother was no longer in the same strong position to control and rebuke, for the Cockneys called her "Mrs Brown" and the French put their own indigenous translation on her relationship with the ghillie and treated him with exaggerated respect.[57] In the event the son went so far as to rebuke his mother.

Alexandra had six children before she was twenty-seven—Albert Victor born in 1864, George in 1865, Louise in 1867, Victoria in 1868, Maud in 1869 and Alexander John in 1871. The three boys were all born prematurely. At the time of the birth of Louise she was suffering from rheumatic fever and thus forbidden the soothing powers of chloroform.[58] After four months in the sickroom, she came back to her gay world with a stiff knee and impaired hearing. The deafness increased with the passing years. By 1871 she was tired out. The quickly succeeding pregnancies, the lameness, the difficulty in hearing, the endless nights when she lay, sleepless, waiting for her husband to return from his pleasures and not allowing herself to take a sleeping draught until she heard his step, all mounted up and took their toll. People talked of Albert Edward's "troop of fine ladies", and in particular of Hortense Schneider.[59]

The death of Alexander John in infancy hit Alexandra very, very hard. There were no more children and it is doubtful whether the conjugal arrangement continued. The Mordaunt divorce case pointed the way of things to come, and the experience of walking into a ballroom and knowing that her husband's mistresses were watching her every move was sufficient grounds for a future Queen to hide herself in her children's love. In the adult merry-go-round she drew her strength from Oliver Montagu, Lord Sandwich's son, and his death in 1893 "left in her heart an aching void which was never filled".[60] Louisa, Countess of Antrim, wrote of this friendship:

> The Princess of Wales floated through this little ballroom world like a vision from fairy-land. She went out a great deal and chief amongst her cavaliers was Oliver Montagu. Her husband by this time was living in a very fast set and indulging in many flirtations. It is surprising that, young and lovely as she was, the Princess never gave any real occasion for scandal. I think it must have been largely due to Oliver Montagu's care for her. He shielded her in every way, not least from his own great love, and managed to defeat gossip. Oliver Montagu was at the top of the social tree in the 70's. He was looked upon with awe by the young as he sauntered into a ballroom regardless of any but his beautiful Princess, who as a matter of course invariably danced the first after supper valse with him. But she remained marvellously circumspect, which was all the more to be wondered at as by that time the Prince's "amours" had several times all but caused her to return to her parents.[61]

Albert Edward has been described as a "lusty lover". The description is as incorrect in his case as it was in that of Henry VIII, who went through wives "as some men go through socks".[62] One of the reasons why Anne Boleyn lost her head was that Henry learned that she had complained of his lack of "staying power".[63] Fertility has no bearing on the point—that cold fish the Prince Consort had nine children. Certain of the Prince's ladies were not discreet, particularly after their sun had set, and Lillie Langtry made her point when she popped a piece of ice from the champagne bucket into the interior of the Prince's clothing, a peccadillo which cost her many months in exile.[64]

The light-hearted approach to sex and the frequent change in bedmates down-graded the value. It became the short answer to boredom, and not to participate was to be out of the swim. Six Edwardian ladies, chatting together over tea, all admitted that they had lovers. A lady's maid at a weekend house-party boasted in the servants' hall that "her lady was the only one to keep her room". What contrast was this with the castigation meted out to Lord Palmerston by Prince Albert for his intrusion into the bedroom of a lady-in-waiting at Windsor.[65] The Prince's affairs were so frequent that the act of straying lost its importance. Even illegitimate children aroused little attention. His immorality became a joke. His niece, Princess Marie Louise, treated it thus. She recalled how, when the Prince was staying in Paris, he coveted a certain pretty girl and laid his plans to pay her a nocturnal visit. The sign was to be a rose outside her door. But, of design, a false trail was laid and H.R.H. ended in the bedroom of a kitchenmaid. Even Queen Mary laughed at this anecdote[66]—no one took Bertie seriously: yet if Queen Mary had been discovered entering the room of a butler, the British Empire would have reverberated. It must have been somewhat difficult for that other Prince of Wales, Queen Mary's eldest son, who was brought up at Sandringham, to understand how the pendulum of the value of sex could swing so far in so few years.

In the days when Albert Edward and Louise Cresswell were young, did the thoughts of one, or both, of them stray out beyond the boundary of the platonic? Certain it is that her friends "ribbed" her about him. Certain it is on her own admission that she received invitations which could have led into the London Season and Marlborough House. Certain it is that she was blissfully happy when she was dancing with him.

They stood together one moonlit, frosty night by the lake at Sandringham, watching the skaters twirling on the ice. He had found her standing alone and apart, and had fetched her a drink. He asked her to come each night that the skating continued. But she did not come back. When next they met, he asked her why.

He was so easily bored and women were an essential to him. She lived alone, but a few fields away. She was tall, attractive and intelligent. She was elusive and she was sad—"lips that taste of tears they say, are best for kissing".[67] She was also authoritarian, and this was a quality which attracted him, as it did others of his ilk.

Her feelings for him were seldom temperate. Either they burned hot or very cold. That they ended in deep hate was a tragedy for both of them. When the Prince lay at death's door in 1871, her anxiety went far beyond that to be expected between tenant and landlord. It was she who, in Sandringham church, presented to the Princess a casket in thanksgiving for his recovery.[68] Her praise for Alexandra is always couched in the superlative. Yet surely the future Queen, if she had been so minded, could have saved the tenant from the fate of having her treasured possessions and beloved animals sold in auction, her life disrupted, as she went into exile?

To find the answer one must read carefully between lines written nearly a century ago.

SOURCES

1   Fulford: *Dearest Child*, p. 147
2   Ibid.
3   Corti: *The English Empress*, p. 54
4   Martin: *Life of the Prince Consort*, Vol. I, p. 316
5   *Letters of Queen Victoria*, 1st December 1841
6   Corti: *The English Empress*, p. 29
7   Ibid.
8   *Dearest Child*, p. 174
9   *Letters of the Prince Consort*, 22nd November 1861
10 Corti: p. 8; Fulford: *Dearest Mama*, p. 30
11 Magnus: *King Edward the Seventh*, p. 300
12 Sykes: *Four Studies in Loyalty*, p. 38
13 Battiscombe: *Queen Alexandra*, p. 24
14 Ibid., p. 86
15 Ponsonby: *The Lost Duchess*, p. 62
16 Ibid., p. 137
17 Lee: *Queen Victoria*, p. 138
18 Magnus: *King Edward the Seventh*, p. 15
19 *Dearest Child*, p. 191
20 Ibid.
21 Ibid., p. 164
22 Barnett Smith: *Life of Queen Victoria*, p. 167
23 *Letters of Queen Victoria*, 6th November 1839
24 *The Early Years of the Prince Consort*, p. 366
25 Longford: *Victoria R.I.*, p. 159
26 Duff: *Albert and Victoria*
27 *Correspondence of Lady Lyttelton*, p. 327
28 Magnus: *King Edward the Seventh*, p. 17
29 Benson: *King Edward VII*, p. 18
30 Magnus: *King Edward the Seventh*, p. 26
31 Ibid., p. 25
32 Corti: *The English Empress*, pp. 50–1
33 *Diary of F. W. Gibbs*
34 Magnus: *King Edward the Seventh*, p. 420

35 Ibid., p. 142
36 "J.P.J.": *Reminiscences*, p. 49
37 Wortham: *The Delightful Profession*, p. 173
38 Sykes: *Four Studies in Loyalty*, p. 29
39 Anon: *Uncensored Recollections*, p. 156
40 Sykes: *Four Studies in Loyalty*, p. 34
41 Magnus: *King Edward the Seventh*, p. 140
42 Wortham: *The Delightful Profession*, p. 254
43 Magnus: *King Edward the Seventh*, p. 143
44 Lee: *King Edward VII*, Vol. I, p. 184
45 Magnus: *King Edward the Seventh*, p. 143
46 Ibid., p. 127
47 Wortham: *The Delightful Profession*, p. 175
48 *Illustrated London News*
49 Benson: *As We Were*, p. 215
50 Shore: *The Baccarat Case*; Wortham, pp. 225–38; Magnus, pp. 279–86
51 Wortham: *The Delightful Profession*, p. 105
52 Magnus: *King Edward the Seventh*, p. 164
53 Ibid., p. 131
54 Duff: *Victoria Travels*, pp. 90–3
55 Marquess of Carisbrooke
56 *George IV: Prince of Wales; Edward—The Uncrowned King*
57 Crawford: *Victoria, Queen and Ruler*, p. 326
58 Battiscombe: *Queen Alexandra*, p. 82
59 Ibid., p. 97
60 Magnus: *King Edward the Seventh*, p. 204
61 Antrim: *Recollections*, p. 221
62 Baldwin Smith: *Henry VIII: The Mask of Royalty*
63 Ibid.
64 Gerson: *Lillie Langtry*, p. 75
65 Duff: *Albert and Victoria*, p. 171
66 *My Memories of Six Reigns*, p. 163
67 Dorothy Parker
68 Sanderson: *King Edward VII*, Vol. II, p. 175

3
The Cresswells

When Gerard Cresswell fell in love with Louise, gentlemen did not farm. In fact there were few paths open to the sons of the gentry in this twilight zone of our history when, with the Duke of Wellington dead and the Crimean War won, the gathering and combined strength of the railways, steamships, the electric telegraph, the Great International Exhibition and the Prince Consort, was pushing the country towards a dreamland of progressive industrialisation and, it was hoped, enlightenment and the easement of the burden for all.

Of course, squires farmed. They managed their own estates and some of them did it very well and made worthy contributions to agriculture. In Norfolk there were the examples to follow of Mr Coke, later created Earl of Leicester, who had brought about an agricultural revolution at Holkam; and the Marquess of Townshend who, in the times of George I, had introduced new methods at Raynham and proved the merit of the turnip.

Yet there was a wide gulf between the squirearchy and the professional farmers, as indeed there was between each of the many layers or classes which made up country life. Each man to his own "pub", and the farmers were determined that there should be no infiltration of their ranks.

On the principle that one could be "genteel and brew, but could not be genteel and bake", a man could farm his own lands, but it was socially taboo, and almost unheard of, for a gentleman to attempt to make a living by tenant-farming. It was also financial suicide, as the *bona fide* farmers had control of the hired lands and considered that competition for them among themselves was fierce enough without additional interlopers from the Hall or Manor. Thus very few young men received the chance to start on this hard furrow. And even if they did, they were handicapped by the almost insurmountable task of obtaining knowledge and experience. There were no agricultural colleges or academic sources of information. So the would-be agriculturalist had to turn to the practising farmer for advice. As the farmer considered the experiment against his interests, he either held back information or, if under pressure, passed on plausible but spurious data. The dealers and the salesmen took delight in outwitting the student. The workers on the farm regarded him as an interloper, even as a spy, and hence a series of mysterious accidents and disasters would become his lot. The general result in such cases was that the young optimist gave up the unequal struggle and returned home, to be received by the chorus of "We told you so" from his relatives. Thereafter he confined his efforts to make a living to the orthodox openings allowed to one of his station—the army or navy, the Church or the law, or, if he was still daring, country banking.

In those days the advantages of life were definitely with the elder sons, sheltering under the umbrella of inheritancy and first choice. Smaller and smaller became the slices of cake as newcomers arrived in nurseries, the only concession to family planning being the eventual physical exhaustion of Mamma at around the age of thirty-eight. Gerard was a younger son of a younger son, although he was fortunate in that his father was a banker.

Louise came in for the then customary parental opposition when she announced that she was going to marry a younger son. She had spent much of her time in London and was accustomed to the good life and the care of a lady's maid. Her brother was a Master of Foxhounds in the Shires and it had been hoped that she would marry a man with inherited prospects. But she was ever a woman prepared to stand on her own two feet and, once her mind was made up, nothing would change it. She wrote:

> Oh! the hearts that have been broken for younger sons! Why should the British matron hold them in such terror? No true love match came to grief yet. England, I admit, will not do for very small incomes, and it is not pleasant to be everybody's poor relation, but there are plenty of other and more sensible countries where it is no disgrace to be your own head cook and housemaid.[1]

Socially, the Cresswells were beyond reproach. There was a touch of vinegar in Louise's description of them:

> . . . one of those old historic families still to be found near the Scottish Borders, who have lived on the same estates and called them after their own names from such remote antiquity that it would not be surprising if they were one day honoured with a special Act of Parliament for the purpose of dividing their inheritance among

their retainers, upon the grounds that they have enjoyed them quite long enough . . .[2]

Certain it was that one could trace them back through six centuries of time. Sir Roger de Cresswell lived in the reign of King John. John de Cresswell "received in 1386 from King Richard II in discharge of arrears due to his father, a grant of many portions of land in the county of Northumberland, to be held by the yearly payment of one white greyhound".[3] There was a claim to royal connection. In the time of Henry VIII, Robert married Elizabeth, "daughter of Sir Thomas Lumley, by Elizabeth Plantagenet his wife, daughter of King Edward IV and the Lady Elizabeth Lucy".[4] But doubts have been expressed about that.[5]

In 1768 came tragedy. John married Catherine Dyer. He was only nineteen. Catherine gave birth to twin girls, but died three weeks later. The elder twin, Frances, married Francis Easterby, who assumed the surname and arms of Cresswell in 1807. They had five sons, outstanding amongst whom was Sir Cresswell Cresswell, a distinguished figure in the sphere of law. Called to the Bar in 1819, he entered Parliament as Conservative member for Liverpool in 1837. In 1842 he was made a Judge of the Court of Common Pleas and was knighted. In 1858 he became the first Judge of the new Court for probate, divorce and matrimonial causes.

The Judge's brother, Francis, married into a most interesting family. His wife was Rachel Fry, daughter of the prison reformer. And Elizabeth was a Gurney.

The Gurney line can be traced back to even earlier times than can the Cresswells. They were a Normandy family—Hugo de Gournay came over with William the Conqueror and was granted manorial rights in East Anglia. Banking claimed their interest from early in the seventeenth century, and John Gurney, born in 1655, embraced the tenets of the Quakers and joined the Society of Friends.

Another John, of Norwich, who died in 1809, left four sons and seven daughters, and "rarely does a family yield in one generation five such splendid characters".[6] Samuel and Daniel were bankers and philanthropists. Samuel took over the family business and then branched out in London. He took over control of Richardson, Overend & Co., a house which devoted itself exclusively to trade in bills. At the time bill-discounting was carried on in a spasmodic fashion by merchants and the specialised service proved an immediate success. The name of the firm was changed to Overend, Gurney & Co., and "for forty years was the greatest discounting house in the world". Samuel used his great worth to further philanthropic aims and on his death in 1856 left a great and flourishing business, known as "the banker's bank". Ten years later it failed, with liabilities amounting to eleven millions sterling.[7]

Daniel remained a leading light in Norfolk banking for sixty years. Joseph John was the academic brother, writing on classical themes before entering the Quaker ministry. His work took him over all the world. He was staunch friend of the slaves and a campaigner for prison reform.

They had seven sisters—Catherine, Rachel, Elizabeth, Richenda, Hannah, Louisa and Priscilla. Auburn hair predominated among them. They wore scarlet coats and purple boots and they attracted considerable attention in Norwich as they made their way to the Quaker Chapel in Goat Lane, known to the girls by the nickname of "Goats". All were talented and John Crome came to Earlham Hall to teach them drawing.[8]

Elizabeth was the star among them. At twenty she married Joseph Fry, a rich London merchant, and devoted herself to her aim of improving the lot of prisoners. She became a frequent visitor to Newgate and in 1817 formed an Association for the improvement of the living conditions of the women confined there. She inspected prisons throughout Britain and Europe and became the leading authority of her time. She had a numerous family, among whom was Rachel, who married Francis Cresswell. Francis, of natural course, became a banker. Their King's Lynn home was the old Bank House, on King Staithe Quay, built in the eighteenth century and carrying a statue of Charles I in a niche on the brick façade.[9]

Francis—Gerard Cresswell's father—was Mayor of Lynn in 1845 and a street was named after him. He died in 1861. He was a member of the bank known as "Gurneys, Birbeck, Barclay, Buxton & Cresswell", with head office at Tuesday Market Place, Lynn. Louise had interesting comment to make on these finance houses which, for good reason, she came to know very well:

> These Banks are a very old Norfolk institution, and different to anything of this kind in the kingdom. Founded originally by a well-known and powerful family of Quakers, they have gradually spread over the county until there is hardly a town of any importance without a branch establishment located there. The partners of the last generation kept to the faith of their fathers, and with the peculiar dress and phraseology of their creed, formed a distinct

colony in the neighbourhood of Norwich, and were noted for the astuteness and skill, in amassing enormous wealth, which seems to be a second nature to the descendants of a persecuted race. It is said that Rothschild of that day declared that his contemporary, the head of the Quaker firm, was more than a match for two Jews, and that if they were shut up over-night, the Jews would be gone before morning, but his "friends"—left alive. The calmness, self-restraint, and power of gauging the weaknesses of their fellowmen without a sign of betrayal, or perhaps contriving to convey the impression that *they* were the weaker vessel, gave them an immense advantage in their intercourse with the outer world; neither were they above "stooping to conquer" and sacrificing pride, temper, or any other "besetment" for the purpose of gaining the object in view, which consequently they rarely failed to obtain; and I have always thought that the versatility and other prominent characteristics of the late Bishop Wilberforce . . . arose from his early intercourse and intimacy with these remarkable people.[10]

Francis and Rachel had a numerous family, one of whom was destined to take his place in the history books. His name was Samuel Gurney Cresswell and he was a member of a naval expedition which sailed to the Arctic in search of the ships of Sir John Franklin. For nearly four poignant years his parents waited for news of him, not knowing whether he was alive or dead. In 1853 Lieutenant Cresswell returned home safely, to the delight of all Lynn. Although he brought back no news of the fate of Sir John, he was the first to be able to confirm that the North-West Passage did, in fact, exist.*

There followed the presentation of a Testimonial to Lieutenant Cresswell:

> On Wednesday, 26th October, the ancient borough of King's Lynn was thrown into excitement, from its being the day chosen to present to this gallant officer a Testimonial from the Mayor, Alder-

---

* Sir John Franklin's expedition to discover the North-West Passage sailed from Greenhithe in May 1845. His two ships were last seen at the entrance to Lancaster Sound at the end of July. Fourteen years passed before the tragic fate of the expedition was uncovered. Lieutenant Cresswell took part in an unsuccessful rescue operation in 1848. In 1850 he sailed again, on *Investigator*, commanded by Captain M'Clure. Six months later *Investigator* rounded Point Barrow, no ship having previously sailed east of this Point. After three grim winters, Captain M'Clure, frozen up in Mercy Bay, entrusted Lieutenant Cresswell with his despatches and instructed him to take twenty-seven sick members of the crew and make the best way he could to Dealy Island, where *Resolute* lay. Cresswell covered the one hundred and seventy miles to Dealy Island without casualty, but his men were in no state to undertake the next stage of the journey home—the three hundred miles to Beechy Island. Cresswell went on his way with a sledge-party from *Resolute*, reaching the island at the end of June. He delivered M'Clure's despatches at the Admiralty on 7th October 1853.

men, and burgesses, indicative of their high sense of the importance
of the tidings of which he had been the bearer, and his own personal
share in the discovery of the North-West Passage. Three o'clock
was the appointed hour, but long before that time the booming of
cannon, the merry ringing of the fine peel of St. Margaret's, and
the flags floating from tower and mast-head, betokened the approaching ceremonial. The Guildhall was prepared for the occasion, and
most beautifully decorated—the north end being covered by flags
tastefully displayed, while in the midst hung the Standard of Old
England. Laurels were wreathed around them, and in the centre
were the initials "S.G.C." formed in dahlias. Beneath these decora-
tions a platform was raised for the Mayor and Corporation, and
the hero of the day; surrounded with seats for the ladies, and the
immediate friends of Lieut. Gurney Cresswell. Every place was
occupied, and the mass behind the barrier swayed to and fro from
the pressure behind them. . . .[11]

The cream of Norfolk society was there that day to honour the
name of Cresswell. They were an august lot and many of them
were soon to be Louise's relations by marriage. But they figured
little in the reminiscences of her life. When she fell in love, she
followed the custom and belief of all the young who fall in love
—hers was the world and she and Gerard its population. Together
they discussed the all important question of how they should spend
their years together. They decided to farm.

> We felt that with our love of horses, dogs, sport and country life
> in all its branches, any other existence would be quite unendurable,
> and not choosing to vegetate upon an inconveniently small income,
> or sink into that most object position, the family poor relation and
> pauper, and hoping that we might prove an exception to the rule
> of failures, we decided to make farming our future calling and
> state in life.[12]

Horses were the outstanding interest of both of them, and it
was this interest which swayed their decision. They wished to
breed and train them and, with an acumen ahead of their time,
they appreciated that the provision of the necessary hay and oats,
and the labour about the stables, could be absorbed in the farm
accounts. It then became necessary for Gerard to receive agricultural training and here he was fortunate in being able to call upon
the family banking background in the selection of a suitable and
trustworthy mentor. A Mr Broome, who farmed a few miles east
of King's Lynn, was selected. It was to prove a wise choice, for
farmer Broome was to emerge as the adviser, friend and strong
right arm of Louise through the eighteen full, and often troubled,
years which lay ahead.

SOURCES

1　Cresswell: *Norfolk and the Squires*, etc., p. 21
2　Cresswell: *Eighteen Years on Sandringham Estate*, p. 11
3　*Burke's Landed Gentry*, 1914
4　Ibid.
5　Clive: *This Sun of York*, p. 96
6　Mee: *Norfolk*, p. 105
7　Ibid., *Encyclopaedia Britannica*
8　Ibid., Harrod and Linnell: *Norfolk*, p. 34
9　Harrod and Linnell: *Norfolk*, p. 50
10　Cresswell, pp. 126–7
11　*Illustrated London News*, 5th November 1853
12　Cresswell, p. 11

4
Love on the Farm

On 24th April 1862, at All Saints Church, Knightsbridge, by
the Rev Oswald Cresswell, uncle to the bridegroom (assisted by
the incumbent, the Rev William Harness), Gerard Oswin Cresswell Esq., Sedgeford Hall, Norfolk, son of the late Francis
Cresswell, King's Lynn, to Louisa Mary, youngest daughter of
William Hogge Esq., of Thornham, Norfolk, and of Biggleswade,
Beds.[1]

He was twenty-five and she was thirty-one. It was an exciting
home-coming, for Gerard had, shortly before, become tenant of a
small farm and the newly-weds were starting the adventure
together. They drove twelve miles north-north-east from Lynn and,
from a rise, looked down on a village in a valley. A windmill kept
sentinel upon a hill and through the valley a stream meandered.
Rising above the treetops like a hat with foliage circling its wide
rim was the round Norman tower of the Church of St Mary.

They reached a high gate, a drive bordering a park, and came
to their new home, Sedgeford Hall, built with yellow brick in the
time of Queen Anne and mellowed into beauty with the passing
of the years. The ceilings were low and friendly, and the walls
were panelled. It had been rented furnished. Hand in hand, the
honeymooners ran from room to room, along the passages and up
the stairs, she allotting uses, moving furniture to suit her taste.
Then they set about unpacking the cases of wedding presents
which they had brought with them from London, placing ornaments and vases and pictures until Louise was able to announce
that the place was "liveable".[2] These were moments of real,
ecstatic happiness that she was to carry in her mind for ever. The
interlude at Sedgeford Hall was to be her most precious memory.

It was an auspicious start to a farming career, and a baptism
far exceeding in comfort and convenience that to be expected by
the majority of young couples in like circumstances. Sedgeford
Hall was the dower-house of the Neville-Rolfes of Heacham Hall

and, in the absence of the owner, was let with the park and Home farm. The bailiff lived in a nearby cottage and the farm was handy to the house but hid from sight by a belt of shrubs and trees. The Swiss dairy, which opened into the garden, was gay with painted windows and Dutch tiles. It was a perfect site for a working honeymoon.

But Louise was soon to find that it was one thing to arrive in a Norfolk village, and quite another thing for the village to accept that she had arrived. There has always been a sense of isolationism in Norfolk, and it still survives today. Then a parish was a world in itself and "strangers" began at the parish boundary. Few people read newspapers and a photograph was a family treasure. As an indication of the paucity of letters, Her Majesty's mail for North Norfolk left Thetford at three o'clock in the morning in a one-horse cart and travelled the forty miles to Blakeney. Mail bags were dropped on the way and horses changed at East Dereham.[3]

Before the arrival of the West Norfolk junction railway the only link between Sedgeford and town life was a carrier's cart which ran to the "Green Dragon" at Lynn on Tuesdays. Yet there was a sense of completeness, for the village boasted a grocer and a draper, a baker and a basket maker, a tailor and a shoe maker, a miller and a furniture dealer, a market gardener and a retailer of beer.[4] There was work for the men on the farms and at the mill, in the sand pit and the chalk quarry, and many spent a long life here and felt no urge to stray further than a cart's range. But life was hard, and at harvest time the scythes cut on until the sparks from the rubbing stones showed in the darkness, and the "gleaning bell" called the women to the fields at eight in the morning and sent them home at seven in the evening. As an old man said of his childhood, as the century changed:

> But, laws, times ain't now like what they wuz then. I ha' lived fifty year on one farm, driving a tamer*, allust worked fifteen hours a day, and never had a day's illness o' my life. But now my *disjestment* is the only *failment* I hev. Wages? you ask! I ha' known So-and-so bring up a family and druv a tamer on 7s. 6d. a week. Taturs was what we chiefly lived on—an' great 'uns an all they were, the land fared as tho' that would grow more than tuddo now. . . . Ah, bor, I ha' many a time bought a red herrin' and cut 'im into seven pieces. Ain't that right, John?'[5]

It was, therefore, only natural that differences of outlook between the indigenous population and newcomers centred on

* Team of horses.

matters economic. It was the rule that old potatoes had to be finished up before a start was made on the new, and there was pride in who would grow the longest runner bean, quantity being more vital than taste. If, in the summertime, children grew tired of rhubarb and custard, they were offered the alternative of custard and rhubarb. And the berries on the hedgerows were, to them, the equivalent of the sweets of today.

Louise was quick to find how strong were the battlements of custom. She was accustomed to living well, and she liked to live well, and thus broke many a village rule. The leader of the condemnation was the wife of the bailiff, Mrs Rumbles. She was old and she was granite and she stood in her cottage garden and, with obvious satisfaction, beguiled passers-by with tales of the waste that reigned in the kitchen of the Hall, forecasting that financial doom was approaching fast. The domestic staff who ventured by her were lashed and chided and, on their return, related the punishment which they had endured.

So strong was the air of disapproval that emanated from the old woman that for a time Louise considered that discretion was the better part of valour and kept well out of her way. But the attacks on her staff became so fierce that at last she was forced to brave the cottage door and explain to Mrs Rumbles that she had a small private income of her own and that her so called extravagances would not cripple the farm. The explanation was accepted and an armistice signed. But, as we shall see, it was a shared love and sympathy for animals which finally brought the two together, binding them close in loyalty until Mrs Rumbles died.

The criticism was unfortunate in that it exacerbated the "shaking down" period of the inside staff. Louise had had some experience of running a large establishment, where orders were passed down through the channels of the housekeeper and the butler and only accustomed hands dealt with the silver and the china and the wine, but none of the harder task of dealing with a small and heterogeneous staff. This numbered some five—lady's maid, cook, 'tweenies from the village and, of course, the "backus boy".

The lady's maid, accustomed to the whirl of London and the society of the housekeeper's room, was completely lost at Sedgeford. Unable to cope with the language or outlook of the country girls among whom she was confined, she made no attempt to communicate and retired into her shell, a course which riled the girls considerably.

The cook was the chief cause of the ire of Mrs Rumbles. She had previously been a kitchen-maid in a large house, extravagantly run, and, having absorbed the belief that housekeeping merited a certain weekly financial outlay, she remained faithful to that tenet. When Louise, worried by the size of the bills, cut down in one direction, cook quickly upped the cost in another. But the food was good and well served, both above and below stairs.

The between-maids suffered from lack of experience and training. The wedding presents had included a sufficiency of plate and china, but the girls soon converted this into an insufficiency. "It was rather trying sometimes to have bent spoons and a bruised tea-pot, and to hear an occasional crash of our treasures in the dim distance."[6] Louise would willingly have cleaned the plate and dusted the china herself, but her heart lay on the farm and in the stables, and Gerard, very much in love, did not like to ride or break-in young horses without her.

The last of the staff was most certainly not the least in impact. The "backus boy" was an essential in every farm house. He frequented the "back-us" or back kitchen, and his task was to run errands, pump the water, carry the fuel, hold horses, fetch the letters and other minor chores of an indefinable nature. The equivalent of the "turf boy" of Ireland, his mind was a maze of mischief and trickery. He was the butt of the maids and a safety valve for unrequited cooks who had no other male to abuse. These boys were skilled in pitch-and-toss and smoked a hideous mixture of leaves and "ends" discarded from the house. The tool of their trade was the "shet" knife,* which was put to a great number of uses and was highly insanitary.

The first development in the integration of the staff was the submission of the lady's maid. Sheer loneliness forced her to fraternise and she quickly won the admiration of the other maids by making them up bonnets "in the London style" for them. She was not aware of it, but such creations "were considered an unbecoming liberty if worn by any of the lower classes".[7] The effect in Church on Sunday morning was electric and for some time Louise kept well out of the way of the vicar for fear of receiving a lecture on the dangers of temptation and demoralisation.

The hats caused a further reaction. They filled the hearts of the 'tweenies with a sense of uplift and deportment. They began to give orders to the "backus boy" in a superior manner, and this was bitterly resented. He took to "shenanacking", became recalcitrant

* A pocket knife which "shets" (shuts) up.

and played truant. He ganged up with other village boys and, when sent on an errand, would absent himself for hours at a time. The portents were of trouble ahead, and trouble came.

One evening there was not enough meat left for the servants' supper. There was, as Louise later pointed out, an abundance of eggs and bacon, cheese and bread, but the cook, set upon keeping the bills at a certain figure, decided that these were not good enough and despatched the boy to the shop for a leg of mutton. The staff joined together in making the most dire threats of what would happen to him if he dawdled on the way. Right, thinks the boy, they want speed, they shall have it. He left the house carrying his master's spurs. At the nearby cottage he saddled up Mrs Rumbles's donkey and galloped and spurred the poor creature all the way to the shop and back.

In the morning there was a knock on the Hall door and Mrs Rumbles stood without. She was, as Louise noted, boiling with rage. "Come this way, if you please, ma'am," she said, "and see how 'they' have treated my donkey."[8] ("They" was the only epithet by which she deigned to refer to the staff.)

The poor donkey was in a lamentable state, its flanks lacerated by the spurs. For the first time since her arrival at Sedgeford, Louise was really angry, for she could not abide cruelty to animals or children. She laced into the boy and the staff, but, fortunately for her, there arrived on the scene someone more versed in admonition than herself. An elderly, impressive and female Gurney arrived, complete with confidential maid, to spend the day at Sedgeford and generally to set the young couple to rights. Having examined the donkey, she paraded the staff and harangued them one and all, and, in particular, the "backus boy". He was threatened with parental wrath and violence, informed in detail of the terrors which lay ahead for young ruffians of his kind, and in the final verbal claps of thunder came mention of the gallows. The boy, unaccustomed to such mauling, burst into floods of tears and wails. This led to a further strange happening. It concerned a third member of the visiting party—a gipsy boy.

> Our worthy kinswoman had inherited strong philanthropic tendencies from her Quaker ancestry, and among other erratic schemes for the regeneration of the human species, had introduced a thoroughbred gipsy boy into her household and undertaken to cure him of the habits and instincts of his race.[9]

At the time it was fashionable for great ladies to recruit into their retinue youths of non-English origin, in a misguided effort to instil into them the *tariqa*, or way of life, of the chosen. Princess Alice had a Malay boy in attendance upon her. He was the only male, except John Brown, to end "arse uppards" in a ditch with Queen Victoria.[10]

The reverberations of his mistress laying into the "backus boy" proved too much for the mental stability of the gipsy and away he set for the freedom of the open country, leaping the hedges and ditches and seeking the cover of the woods. Louise watched him go and was certain that they would never see him again. But her kinswoman was master of every problem. A posse of agriculturists acquainted with every hide in the area was quickly summoned and hours later he was returned to the carriage in which his mistress waited. The audience which there gathered was treated to an even more gifted display of oratory than had been the lot of the "backus boy". Amid fits of suppressed laughter, old Rumbles was heard to say: "Ah! he's a-catching it now."[11] At the end of this imperfect day, Louise consoled herself with the thought that accidents occasionally happen in even the best regulated families.

Domestic crises apart, life for Louise and Gerard was fun. The farm was too small to occupy their time fully and thus they were able to join in the social round. Invitations poured in for balls, weddings and weekend stays, giving Louise the chance to show off her trousseau, although she was soon to wish that the cost of this most expensive collection had been transferred to her in cash. In fact the luxurious send-off for the pair was in contrast with their humble standing as small farmers. Among their presents was a brougham. When visiting friends, they drove on the box, putting the man and the maid inside. They were enjoying themselves.

In their honeymoon time, their way of life was somewhat of a joke to their friends, and guests who came to Sedgeford found that they had to adjust their ideas of a country weekend. The family dandy arrived, his get-up reminding Louise of Rotten Row in the Season. After Church on Sundays there was the customary inspection of the "estate". They came to the farmyard. There rested the Cresswell sow. She was a peaceful creature, producing enormous litters, achievements which caused Louise's brothers-in-law to comment that they were the farm's only profit. Hitherto the sow had remained oblivious to inspection, but on this Sabbath she suddenly broke into a charge reminiscent of that of the Gadarene swine. Her course took her between the legs of the dandy. He ended in the black and greasy oozings of the muck-heap. Thereafter his interest in agricultural pursuits ceased abruptly.

But it only too soon became apparent that the necessities of life did not flow from a few acres, the end-products of a sow and the occasional sale of a young horse. It was time for Gerard to move on to wider acres. During the summer a letter arrived from the owner of the Sandringham estate. It informed him that, out of many applicants, he had been chosen to be the tenant of nine-hundred acre Appleton Farm. The owner of Sandringham was a friend of the Cresswells. His name was the Hon. Charles Spencer Cowper and he was the stepson of Lord Palmerston, the Prime Minister.

SOURCES

1 *Lynn Advertiser and West Norfolk Herald*
2 Cresswell, p. 12
3 Marcon : *Reminiscences of a Norfolk Parson*, p. 34
4 *Kelly's Directory*
5 Marcon : *Reminiscences of a Norfolk Parson*, p. 12
6 Cresswell, p. 13
7 Ibid., p. 14
8 Ibid., p. 16
9 Ibid., p. 17
10 *More Leaves from a Journal of a Life in the Highlands*, 7th October 1863
11 Cresswell, p. 18

5
The Foundations of Sandringham

The Romans built villas at Sandringham. Remains may be seen in the museum there. Catus Decianus, Procurator of the province of the Iceni in the reign of Claudius Caesar, introduced a work-force of Belgae to build earthen banks to enclose the fen-lands and the marshes. Catus was the man who scourged Queen Boadicea, and did worse by her daughter.[1] Thus began the royal connections of north-west Norfolk in the Christian era. Thereafter Kings and Queens were thin upon the ground until the time of a benefactor of Lynn, King John, who carelessly lost his treasures through a miscalculation of the tides of the Wash. In the following century Queen Isabella, "the she-wolf of France" and mother of Edward III, lived for some thirty years at Castle Rising.[2] Henry VIII hunted in Norfolk and, in contrast, padded barefoot to Walsingham to pray for the life of his infant son. He also married —and beheaded—a Norfolk girl, Anne Boleyn. Their daughter, Elizabeth I, made a tour of East Anglia in 1578 and commented that she had found such goodwill in Norfolk that she would remember it for all of her life.[3] Charles II was less complimentary, being of the opinion that "Norfolk ought to be cut out into strips to make roads for the rest of the kingdom".[4]

The Hanovers, in the main, neglected the county but there was a rousing reception for a sixteen-year-old girl, afterwards to be Queen Victoria, who arrived at Lynn on the evening of 22nd September 1835. She sought refuge in the Duke's Head inn from the cheering crowds before continuing her journey to Holkham.[5] She was dozing with tiredness as, in the twilight, she passed through the policies of Sandringham, the home that her eldest son, and his son and grandson after him, were to love and cherish.

Before Sandringham swallowed up Appleton, there was long

rivalry between the two estates. Clear records of the houses began in the sixteenth century. In 1517 the Cobbes, a leading Norfolk family, bought Sandringham. They were staunch Catholics and suffered all the fears and threats of religious persecution when Elizabeth came to the Throne. The Bishop of Norwich was ordered to carry out a purge of recusants[6] and two of the Cobbes were on the danger list of those who refused to attend worship at their parish church.[7] Jesuits arriving from the Continent in the Popish "fifth column" knew that there were "safe" houses in the Lynn area, but one who was unfortunate enough to be captured was tortured and executed.

At this time the Pastons, of *Paston Letters* fame, took advantage of the religious trend to increase their property empire, gaining official blessing by building on Popish land which had been desecularised.[8] Sir Edmund Paston began the construction of a house at Binham, on Priory ground granted to his father by Henry VIII. But when a wall collapsed upon a workman, killing him, Sir Edmund feared that there might be further psychic expressions of the anger of Rome, and transferred his plans to Appleton. Then followed Appleton's years, for the new house which arose there outshone Sandringham in both size and beauty—"a very agreeable and handsome pile".[9] The Pastons loved Appleton Hall and lived there until 1707 when it was demolished by fire—but for a watchful shepherd, those who slept there would have been burned in their beds.[10] The now homeless Pastons moved to Wiltshire, but they left their mark in the foundations and grounds of Appleton and traces of their occupation may be seen today.

Meantime Sandringham had changed hands. In 1686 the Cobbes sold to a Dutch family named Hoost, which had become Hoste on settlement in Norfolk. Stones to their memory lie neat in the churchyard of St Mary Magdalene. The Hostes added the Appleton lands on the departure of the Pastons and built there a rambling house sufficient for the needs of a tenant farmer. By the middle of the eighteenth century there was but one Hoste left, a daughter named Susan. She married Cornish Henley, who obligingly assumed the additional name of Hoste, thus continuing his wife's family connection with Sandringham.[11] Cornish rebuilt the Hall, and it stood for one hundred years. It was "a plain but comfortable Georgian structure with a stucco exterior, slate roof and small gables on either front".[12] The last of the Hoste Henleys died in the reign of King William IV and when the Sandringham estate was put up for auction in 1836 it fetched £76,000. The price was interesting, as indeed was the purchaser.

His name was John Motteux and he owned an estate at Beechamswell near Swaffham. The interest lay in the point that he was a friend of the Lambs, and to be in the confidence of that family was a matter of importance, as William Lamb, Viscount Melbourne, was Prime Minister, and his sister, Emily Mary, Lady Cowper, was the love in the life of Lord Palmerston, the Foreign Secretary. Earl Cowper died in 1837 and two years later Palmerston married his "Emmy", to the amusement of young Victoria and Albert who considered that for two people in their fifties to be in love was most odd.[13] By her first marriage "Emmy" had five children, but whether her husband sired them all is open to doubt, as the Lamb ladies were free with their favours. It was rumoured indeed that Palmerston was the father of the youngest son, Charles Spencer, born in 1816.

Earl Cowper was rather a bore and "Emmy" welcomed the visits of John Motteux, who was an amusing conversationalist. Further reasons for encouragement were that he was a bachelor, very rich and with no one in particular to whom to leave those riches. Motteux, for his part, welcomed the social distinction which he gained from the friendship with the Lambs and, as is not unusual when an elderly bachelor is given entrance to a family circle, he made a particular favourite of one of the children. The one that he chose was the above-mentioned Charles Spencer. Palmerston, for stronger reasons, made the same choice, and Charles Spencer was introduced to the Foreign Office and appointed Secretary to the Legations at Florence and Stockholm.

The Hon. Charles Spencer Cowper was a rake. He played cards at Crockford's and lived beyond his modest means. One evening by the fire at Windsor, during the April-October union of Prime Minister and girl-Queen which formed one of the sweetest and most rewarding vignettes of our history, Melbourne told Victoria of his nephew's adventures. He said that he found them "very refreshing".[14] She did not agree, but she still asked him to Windsor, for, inside herself, she leaned towards the naughty men in her life.

John Motteux did not live at Sandringham. He pottered about the gardens and planted fruit trees, increased its area from 5,400 to 7,000 acres and ringed the estate with a fence. He died in 1843.[15]

At that time Spencer Cowper was in Stockholm, which had the advantage of being a good distance from the many in London to whom he owed money. It was his custom on receiving letters which he knew by long experience contained threats from lawyers, to put them on one side and pretend that they had not arrived. This procedure he followed when a suspicious envelope arrived for him one August morning in 1843.[16] Shortly afterwards there followed a series of letters of a very different character. To his amazement, they contained congratulations on his inheriting of the Sandringham and Beechamswell estates under the will of John Motteux. Spencer retrieved the relevant envelope and learned the happy truth. He resigned his appointment and hurried back to London.

As he was now the owner of wide estates, but had little income and many debts, he sold Beechamswell and rented a house in London. Sandringham he retained for its sporting attractions, but Norfolk saw little of him as he spent much of his time in Paris. There he lived the gay life and the general comment of his friends was that it was time he found a wife. This he did in 1852.[17]

It was typical of Spencer Cowper that he should choose a bride who was front page news for the press of Europe. She was the widowed Countess D'Orsay, widely known as "the virgin wife". Not that she was a virgin by the time of her second marriage, as she had surrendered that status to a member of the Royal Family of France. Born Lady Harriett Gardiner in 1812, she was the only legitimate daughter of the Earl of Blessington. Her mother died when Harriett was a child and her father then married Marguerite St Leger Farmer. Marguerite, Countess of Blessington, authoress, was farouche, beautiful, witty and extravagant, but a heartless step-mother to Harriett. In 1822 the Blessingtons, in debt, set out for Italy, leaving the girl at school in Ireland. At Valence they met Alfred, Count D'Orsay, an adventurous dandy accomplished in the arts, and Marguerite fell in love with him. The Count accepted the invitation to accompany the Blessingtons to Italy and in Naples an establishment was set up under a strange tripartite agreement. Lord Blessington did not appear to understand what was afoot, and the exits and entrance of Lord Byron further complicated matters. Fearing that he had not long to live, Blessington made a will by which Harriett was to receive his Irish estates provided that she married Count D'Orsay. The Count was quick to take advantage of this and the girl was fetched from Ireland and married to him when she was fifteen.

Callers at the house saw a sad and demure little girl in a pinafore sitting at one end of the room while her so-called husband flirted with her step-mother at the other.[18] It was a degrading experience which clouded her whole life. Her father died in 1829 and, after three more miserable years, she left her step-mother and husband and settled in Paris. It was there that she was "taken up" by one of the most eligible young men in France, the Duke of Orleans, eldest son of King Louis Philippe.[19] Orleans had been considered as a husband for Princess Victoria, but the plump and inexperienced girl was far from his conception of a female companion. He was horrified at the manner in which she bolted her soup. He was very tall, and she was very small, bringing from him the comment that, if she was to be put into one of his riding boots, she would scarce be able to see over the top. He feared that the people of Paris would burst into fits of laughter at the sight of them standing side by side.[20] An heir for France being necessary, he married elsewhere and obliged, but that did not lessen Harriett's grief when, five years later, he jumped from a runaway carriage, landed on his head and was killed.[21] Soon afterwards she met Spencer Cowper, spreading his new found wealth about Paris. Her ethereal beauty captivated him and they were married after D'Orsay's death in 1852. They came to Sandringham and a daughter was born. The child, Mary, was with them in Paris in September 1854 when a cholera epidemic broke out. The Cowpers left at once for Dieppe and home, but Mary was already infected and died at the Hotel de Dieppe. The tragedy engulfed the mother. She bought all the furniture in the room in which Mary had died and, on her return to Sandringham, arranged a *chapelle ardente*, in much the same fashion as the Princess of Wales was to do forty years later on the death of her eldest son, the Duke of Clarence. The spirit had gone out of her and she turned to religion for comfort. In 1855 she restored Sandringham's Church of St Mary Magdalene[22] and placed there a memorial tablet to Mary. She opened an orphanage in a nearby farmhouse and every day taught the children and walked with them in the park.[23] She was a portrait of sadness and Louise Cresswell, who knew her well, wrote of her:

> Why sorrow and sin should have been sent to one born to the gifts of rank, wealth and marvellous beauty, is a mystery that we cannot attempt to penetrate. To those who heard from her own lips the sad story of her life, and the terrible cruelty of her early wrongs, it was impossible not to feel the injustice which she never seemed to feel for herself, that the author of her misery should have been courted and idolised to the last, leaving her to repent in sackcloth and ashes.[24]

The contemporary situation was in marked contrast with the way of life to which Spencer Cowper had been accustomed, and which he favoured, as his subsequent career proved. He escaped to Paris when the opportunity arose and once again the bogey of finance appeared before him. His mother and Palmerston decided that something must be done to avert a catastrophe. Palmerston, now Prime Minister, developed a neat little plan. He would canalise back to the needy Lambs a considerable portion of the moneys piled up by Prince Albert since his arrival, as a near penniless princeling from Coburg, twenty-three years before.

SOURCES

1   *London Society*, Vol. II, 1862
2   Hutchison: *Edward II*, p. 144
3   Williams: *The Life and Times of Elizabeth*
4   *London Society*, Vol. II, 1862
5   Duff: *Victoria Travels*, p. 48
6   Plowden: *Danger to Elizabeth*, p. 108
7   Cathcart: *Sandringham*, p. 41
8   Ibid.
9   Blomefield & Parkin: *History of Norfolk*
10 Le Neve
11 Cathcart: *Sandringham*, pp. 46–50
12 *Sandringham: A Guide to the Grounds*, etc.
13 *Letters of Queen Victoria*, 8th December 1839; *Letters of the Prince Consort*, p. 42
14 Cecil: *Melbourne*, p. 332
15 Cathcart: *Sandringham*, p. 62
16 Watson: *King Edward VII as a Sportsman*, p. 16
17 Cathcart: *Sandringham*, p. 65
18 Jones: *Sandringham—Past and Present*
19 Ibid.
20 Duff: *Albert and Victoria*, p. 93
21 *Letters of Queen Victoria*, 15th July 1842
22 Ashton: *Sandringham Church*, p. 3
23 Jones; Cathcart
24 Cresswell, p. 23

6
Property Deals

In 1852 Prince Albert labelled Lord Palmerston, "the man who has embittered our whole life".[1] But the Prince had the same outlook as had George II, of whom it was said: "Whenever he met with opposition to his designs, he thought the opposers insolent rebels to the will of God."[2]

It was well understandable that Albert should think as he did. Since childhood he had been groomed to be husband of the British Queen, and into his eager brain King Leopold of the Belgians and Baron Stockmar had pumped the message that he was to be the messiah who would take the truth to England, cut down the coronets of the aristocracy to size and join Britain to a unified, liberal minded Germany. Not unnaturally, Palmerston took strong exception to being told what to do by a German student. A mettlesome man, he was not open to advice or interference. He was a senior statesman of the country to which he belonged and had begun his parliamentary career twelve years before Albert was born. Palmerston was Foreign Secretary from 1846–1851 and throughout these five years the two clashed continually over the policy to be adopted towards Europe. "Albert tried every trick in the Coburg book to rid himself of his adversary, even resorting to insinuations regarding his sexual escapades."[3] Although Palmerston was eventually dismissed for his unauthorised recognition of the régime of Napoleon III, he was back again in office next year as Home Secretary and hungry for the blood of those who had toppled him—Albert being chief among them. As the years of the short life of the Queen's husband ran out, the statesman came to appreciate his intrinsic qualities and the brilliance of his over-worked brain. Yet when a man of the ilk of Palmerston made up his mind about a man, there was no going back on it. Not even death could alter it.

Palmerston had a personal reason for a grudge against Albert. This was the treatment meted out to his wife's brother, Lord

Melbourne. Melbourne moulded Victoria into the great Queen which she became. He alone had her ear in the years before her marriage and into that ear he poured an unrivalled wealth of experience and knowledge. He gave her balance and judgment and taught her the value of humanity. She was his last flirtation with life and power—and therefore he was in love with her and his eyes never left her. There was no desire for the physical touch, for he was sixty and the Lambs aged early. She saw more of him in the daylight hours than is the lost of most wives with their husbands and she turned to him for advice on every point. She wept bitterly at the thought of parting and fought to keep him by her side. Her admiration was intense. That the physical entered her feelings was only natural, for it was an integral part of the upsurge of spring.

Albert was an egotistical prig when he arrived in London to marry Queen Victoria. He had anticipated being master of the house and in a position to organise it as he wished. He had no intention that the day would be long delayed when he would be King in all but title. Instead he found his wife's trust and affections firmly bestowed on a man old enough to be his grandfather. It was the suspicion that there had been feelings beyond the platonic which riled the young husband. He referred to the Prime Minister as "the old man" and criticised his "lazy ways" in political direction.[4]

Youth had to win. After Melbourne went out of office in August 1842, he was to all intents forbidden the Palace and even correspondence with the Queen. He refused to comply but, in his abject loneliness, was restrained from taking strong action for fear of losing the friendship of the woman whom he loved. The collapse of his health in 1842 settled the matter, but Albert, in his new found psychological power, was not content until he had wrung from his wife the confession that the years 1837–39 had been full of "an artificial sort of happiness", compared to the "real and solid happiness" she now had with her Beloved Husband.[5] Melbourne lasted six more years, sad and ineffectual in his twilight at Brocket. He relied now for comradeship and help on his sister, Lady Palmerston, and she was with him when he died. She knew well that her brother's efforts and energies to help the young Queen had cost him his health and years of his life. There were no bouquets for Albert from Broadlands.

Albert's love of money, his acumen in obtaining it and his parsimony when spending it, were a source of constant and bitter comment with cartoonists and satirists. The aristocracy, fully aware of the poverty in Coburg, watched the pile mount with a sardonic sneer. Certain it is that Albert was a brilliant property speculator. In each case he worked under the mantle of seeking the advice of senior Ministers. If he could not persuade vendors to reduce their price to the figure he thought fit, he moved into the property under cover of a lease, knowing full well that, once the British Queen was installed, little short of dynamite could evict her. His first success was with the Osborne estate in the Isle of Wight. The total asking price, taking into account development value, was £50,000, at which Sir Robert Peel, then Prime Minister, held up his hands in horror. Albert took a year's lease for £1,000, and then bought the whole place for £26,000.[8] Turning his attention to Scotland, he had immediate success in purchasing the 6,500 acres of Birkhall, at the head of Glen Muick, from the Gordons as a home for the Prince of Wales, but he failed in capturing Abergeldie, where he had to be content with a forty year lease. With his eye on Balmoral he took the advice of Lord Aberdeen, whose brother, Sir Robert Gordon, was the tenant at the time. Sir Robert died in 1847, leaving the way clear.

Here Albert was dealing with men shrewd and experienced in property dealing. Balmoral belonged to the Fifes and was but one of many estates which had come into their hands as a result of the exploitation of the fortune amassed by a wily merchant of Morayshire, William Duff of Dipple. "Dipple", as he was known, "dealed in salmon, meale and grain and greatly in malt", slept in his mill and drank two bottles of claret every day. "Dipple's" son inherited his flair, became Earl of Fife, and Balmoral was bought in 1798 as a property for letting and with an eye for a profit on re-sale.[7]

Albert followed his previous technique of moving in as a tenant but, when he and his wife drove from Aberdeen to Ballater on a September day in 1848, with triumphal arches and receptions all along the way, it was obvious, and certainly hoped, that they had come to stay. Four years passed before Albert could make terms with the Fife Trustees. He complained about their stubbornness, and yet in the end paid only 30,000 guineas for the 17,400 acre estate. It was a bargain indeed, and the purchase was made in his own name. But he had been forced to delay the building of a new Castle and he was still making improvements when the time came for him to begin another property adventure— this time the provision of a home for the Prince of Wales and his bride.

The matter was first considered in 1860 and became a matter

of urgency when Baron Stockmar warned that, if Albert Edward was not provided with a country home and a regular companion at nights, disaster lay ahead for the British Throne.[8] Many properties were considered. The Rev. Charles Kingsley suggested Bramshill in Hampshire and Lord Macclesfield put forward Eynsham in Oxfordshire. Houghton in Norfolk was on the list.[9] Yet in each case difficulties arose—the buildings or site were unsuitable, the price was too high, owners were unwilling to sell. As was his wont, Prince Albert consulted the Prime Minister, who was Lord Palmerston. By strange coincidence Palmerston confided that he knew of the ideal place. It was called Sandringham and was owned by his stepson, who might be persuaded to sell. When the Prince Consort died in December 1861, there were only two properties left on the list—Sandringham in Norfolk and Somerleyton Hall, near Lowestoft in Suffolk, the home of Sir Samuel Morton Peto.[10]

In her abject misery the Queen was most unwilling to see her Ministers. Those who had essential business with her heard her voice only through the open door of the adjacent room. But King Leopold of the Belgians and Lord Grantchester insisted that she see Lord Palmerston, and he travelled to Osborne on 29th January. She dreaded seeing the forceful old man,[11] but she was prompted to do so by her determination to ensure the fulfilment of her wishes. The first of these was that every plan and view of the Prince Consort should be followed exactly. The second was that Bertie should depart from her presence and quickly. Fortunately his father had arranged for him to tour Egypt and the Holy Land, and this was to be the first of the dead man's plans to be fulfilled. It was not only that the sight of the boy sent a shudder of revulsion through her, but also because she saw him as a danger, not so much from his own aspirations but from a possible desire and expectation on the part of the country that he should relieve his mother of some of her duties and take over a piece of the mantle of Albert. That, the Queen determined, would never happen. She wanted time to enable her to take steps to ensure that the rôle of the Heir remained as minor as it had been before.[12] She wrote in her diary on 29th January 1862 :

> After luncheon saw Lord Palmerston (who has been very ill). . . . He seemed very nervous himself. . . . He could in fact hardly speak for emotion. It showed me how much he felt my terrible loss, and he said what a dreadful calamity it was. Then he spoke about Bertie, and the desirability for his travelling, which would be such a good thing for him. I repeated that it had been his father's wish that he should do so; and Lord Palmerston said it was most important

that he should marry. I observed that he was a very good and dutiful son, but that for him, just at his age, the loss of his Father was terrible, which Lord Palmerston thoroughly understands and feels keenly. Every thing was quiet, he thought there would be no trouble, but "*the* difficulty of the moment" was Bertie. I felt the same, and would hardly have given Lord Palmerston credit for entering so entirely into my anxieties. . . . He was most anxious to facilitate things for me. . . .[13]

There were now only nine days left before the tour of Egypt and the Holy Land was due to begin and Palmerston moved quickly. On the morning of 3rd February the Prince travelled to King's Lynn, incognito and by ordinary train. He was accompanied by General Bruce, his Governor, Sir Charles Phipps, Keeper of the Privy Purse, and Mr White, the Crown solicitor. After lunch at the Globe Hotel, the party drove to Sandringham, made their inspection and were introduced to two selected tenants. They were back in Lynn to catch the 4.40 for London, so the inspection of the 7,000 acre estate can at best have been cursory. It was a busy day for the local newspaper reporters, and on the 8th the *Lynn Advertiser and West Norfolk Herald* commented:

Of course nothing is known as to the decision likely . . . but the probability of a nearby Royal residence is causing speculation . . . and even positive assertion.

On 22nd February the official announcement appeared in the national press that the Prince of Wales had concluded the purchase of Sandringham before leaving England. It was specifically stated that it had been bought "for shooting purposes"[14]—an interesting point in view of later happenings. Somerleyton Hall was not given a chance to compete and passed into the hands of Sir Savile Brinton Crossley.

The excitement aroused locally over a royal residence for Norfolk was rivalled by the price paid. This was £220,000. When Sandringham had been auctioned in 1836 it had fetched only £76,000. Although John Motteux had added some thousand acres and Spencer Cowper had made certain structural alterations, the increase in value was hard to explain. Certainly the heart-broken Queen would not have had the spirit or the experience to conduct property business, but she had beside her a most astute financial adviser in the person of her Uncle Leopold. He had been a liability to the British public since his arrival to marry Princess Charlotte and he had invested profitably in property and the fine arts. He had written to his niece from Buckingham Palace on 24th January:

It is undoubtedly your own interest for the sake of having no difficulties, as well as that of the country, that Pilgerstein* and his people should not be upset. I have this very moment written to Pilgerstein to accept me an offer which he has made to run up here and see me, which may be useful to put things as you wish them to be. . . . The Government has but a doubtful majority; to have it upset would be for you and for everybody very unprofitable.[15]

Nor must it be imagined that Sir Charles Phipps was being profligate in the spending of royal moneys, for at the time of the the time of the purchase of Sandringham he was engaged in fierce conflict with the Lord Chamberlain in an attempt to relieve the Queen of the expenses of paying for her mother's funeral, demanding that they come from public funds.[16]

That Lord Palmerston was in clear control of events is obvious. Lady Harriett Cowper said of the sale: "The large sum of money obtained (220,000L.) and the high station of the purchaser were great inducements. . . ."[17]

It was arranged that completion of the purchase should be early in September and that Spencer Cowper should remove his possessions by then. Louise and Gerard were married on 24th April. It is therefore strange that, when they were offered the tenancy of Appleton Farm, they were under the impression that Spencer Cowper would be their landlord. Louise described him as "a perfect landlord, neighbour and friend".[18] Despite the press announcements, despite their close family connection with banking and the fact that the Cowpers were their near neighbours and friends, let alone local gossip, the newly weds were in ignorance of the sale which had been concluded on 22nd February. Perhaps the explanation is that love is blind. Louise commented:

> It was extremely difficult to get a farm at that time, and a vacancy of rare occurrence, and it was very kind of the owner of Sandringham to offer us one on his estate . . . and had it still belonged to him when we migrated there, it might have altered our views as to the prudence of the undertaking; but, to our great regret, it was suddenly sold to the Prince of Wales. . . .[19]

The sudden sale to which she refers was in fact the completion stage and the Cresswells were faced with a *fait accompli*. Although their ignorance is hard to understand, the reason why they were offered the tenancy becomes clearer. When the Prince of Wales made his inspection, two "selected" tenants, neat and brushed,

---

* King Leopold's somewhat uncomplimentary sobriquet for Lord Palmerston
—*Pilger* being German for "palmer".

had been put on parade for his inspection. No one told him, or Sir Charles Phipps, that up at Appleton there lived two dirty and mean old men whose rat-ridden farm was a disgrace to the county. They had reaped a rich financial harvest from the high prices obtaining during the time of the Crimean War and had never ploughed a penny back into the land or the buildings. Nor had they made any demands on the Hon. Spencer Cowper, which doubtless suited him. But now the time had come for them to disappear, and speedily, for if Queen Victoria should suddenly descend on Norfolk and, accustomed as she was to the spotless and highly organised farms of Prince Albert, become bogged down in the muckheaps of the dirty old men of Appleton, the Hon. Spencer would find himself with some awkward explaining to do and probably be excommunicated from Windsor. So Spencer dropped a line to H.R.H. before he left informing him that a delightful and efficient young couple, named Cresswell, were now in control at Appleton and all would soon be shipshape. Louise thought it was very kind of Spencer to "name them" to His Royal Highness.[20]

SOURCES

1 Duke Ernest: *Memoirs*
2 Trench: *George II*, p. 39
3 Duff: *Albert and Victoria*, p. 247
4 Fulford: *Prince Consort*, p. 67
5 Esher: *Girlhood of Queen Victoria*, Vol. II, p. 135
6 Fulford: *Prince Consort*, p. 78
7 Tayler: *The Book of the Duffs*, pp. 104–5
8 Corti: *The English Empress*, p. 72
9 Arthur: *Concerning Queen Victoria and her Son*, p. 113; Cathcart: *Sandringham*, p. 30
10 *Illustrated London News*, 22nd February 1862
11 Connell: *Regina v Palmerston*
12 Duff: *Hessian Tapestry*, p. 75
13 *Letters of Queen Victoria*
14 *Illustrated London News*, 22nd February 1862
15 *Letters of Queen Victoria*
16 Watson: *A Queen at Home*, p. 154
17 Jones: *Sandringham—Past and Present*
18 Cresswell: *Norfolk and the Squires, Clergy*, etc., p. 15
19 Cresswell, p. 22
20 Ibid., p. 29

7
Moving House

Louise did not wish to leave Sedgeford. When the excitement over the offer of the Appleton tenancy had passed, there came upon her a presentiment—a feeling that to move would lead to disaster. She was not a superstitious woman and she could not understand the cold shivers of fear which ran through her.

There were many reasons why she wished to continue living at Sedgeford Hall. First came the lovely Anne house, snug in a village in a valley, aproned by the lush green park. Secondly, there were the treasured memories of a honeymoon summer. High on the list was the very practical reason of security. While Gerard could not make a large profit there, at least he could not make a crippling loss, and losses were the nightmare of the amateur farmer.

Louise put these points to her husband and he passed them on in discussion with his family. Although he may not have been aware of what was afoot at Sandringham, his relations most certainly were. To them the views to which they listened smacked of heresy. To turn down the chance of working side by side with the Heir to the Throne simply was not business. A man must make his way in the world, etc., etc. So the in-laws descended on Sedgeford in force and the assault on Louise began.

> It was a case of being over-ruled and over-persuaded, and it was especially urged upon me that if I influenced my husband in the matter, I should afterwards repent of having kept him in a narrow way of life, without enough to do, and no opportunity of developing his energies.[1]

That she was six years older than Gerard did not make matters easier for her. It was impossible for her to carry through life the accusation that she had held her husband back. She surrendered.

But on one point Gerard was adamant. If the battue system of shooting was to be developed at Sandringham, he would not consider the Appleton tenancy, no matter how low the rent might be.[2] He had good reasons for this decision, for at the time a revolution was taking place on the big estates, not as drastic as the "clearances" in Scotland, but a revolution just the same. The men who had made fortunes out of the railways, coal, engineering and cotton, and grown fatter still on the swollen profits of the Crimean War, were moving into country homes. They had collected titles and become Justices of the Peace. They were in a great hurry to climb the ladder leading to aristocratic heights and, as often happens on such occasions of infiltration, they became more genteel than the gentry and, of course, devoted to their "typical English tea". They splashed out with conservatories and fountains, stable blocks and terraces. While their staff mostly lived well and revelled in their new suburbanised dwellings, the poor folk who lived around were not so happy. Common lands were fenced in, rights of way closed, and, while it was a sin to snare a rabbit, it was sacrilege to touch a pheasant. Ever-watchful *Punch* let fly at the new-comers:

THE NEW LANDED INTEREST

EXTOLLING the mighty works of Commerce, the *Morning Post* indites the following reflection:

"How many of the ancient parks and baronial halls have passed from their old and much encumbered proprietors into the hands of cotton spinners, cotton-brokers, brewers, ironmasters, and engineers, overflowing with ready cash, and boasting gigantic balances at their bankers!"

Yes; and see what a vast improvement has taken place of late years in the character of the landed interest. How much more generous and liberal the new English country gentlemen are than the old English country gentlemen were! Consider in how great a degree, for instance, the modern landlords, the successful speculators and manufacturers by whom the ancient gentry have been happily bought out, have practically, as well as legally, relaxed the Game Laws, which no doubt they will shortly simplify by declaring all game property; in fact, doing away with the distinction between wild and tame creatures altogether. The law of trespass also; how leniently that is enforced by them! Even where the commons, open from time immemorial till lately, have been enclosed, you can go anywhere and do anything so long as you keep in the public highways, and don't go aside into the fields to gather mushrooms or pick flowers. Hurrah for the New Landed Interest![3]

Who, then, were the new rich deposing? Thus Louise described them:

The Squire of the old school—is he disappearing from the scene to return no more? Shall we ever meet him again at the covert side, or see him shouldering his guns up and down the turnips—no new fangled ways of shooting for *him*—or riding round his estate on that perfect old grey cob, or laying down the law, spud in hand, to Giles the steward; in dress not half so swell as some of his own tenants, with provincialisms of speech contracted from addressing the said Giles and his subordinates in their native tongue; the modicum of Greek and Latin picked up at Eton and Oxford, before competitive examinations made brains and bookworms override manliness, forgotten long ago; rejecting modern literature as "trash", untravelled and prejudiced beyond belief—what claim has he but a traditionary one to the social status of a gentleman? Underneath that rough outside you find a kindliness and courtesy, a chivalry and honour *"sans peur et sans reproche"*; so true and just in all his dealings, scorning the sharp practice and lies of modern commerce as unworthy of his ancestral shield, bringing up his children to "fear God" and "honour the King", verily, we may be proud of him, for nowhere but in the British Isles do we ever find his like[4]

The battue was fast becoming the "done thing" with the *jeunesse dorée* and Gerard had no intention of running a game farm for their convenience. He took farming seriously. He was not against shooting as a sport and relaxation, but he knew only too well that the Germanised version introduced by Prince Albert would bring about his ruin. Albert had showed his taste when he rounded up the herd of deer at Osborne and invited his cronies to shoot them down, as he feared that they might damage his lawns and flowerbeds. His idea of shooting was to bag as much game as possible with the maximum of efficiency in the shortest possible time. Of course the breech-loader helped. When he married Queen Victoria, shooting in England was a modest and gentlemanly pursuit, two or three guns, a loader and a couple of setters being considered sufficient for a satisfactory day's sport. As Roger Fulford commented: "The huge shooting-party with hordes of minions, the 'slap-up' luncheon and the minimum of exercise, beloved by the best county families of Surrey, had not as yet made its expensive appearance."[5] But the rich industrialists admired Albert to the same degree that the aristocracy despised him, and they followed in his ways and enriched them. Louise and Gerard had seen signs of the trend in Norfolk and decided to tackle their new landlord on the point before signing anything.

To some extent they became the victims of exciting contemporary events. On 30th August the following appeared in the Court column of the *Illustrated London News*:

The marriage of the Prince of Wales with the Princess of Denmark will be celebrated early in the ensuing spring. General Knollys . . . has been appointed Comptroller of the Household of his Royal Highness, and Marlborough House is being prepared as quickly as possible for his reception.

This apparently authoritative announcement was dynamite, as the Queen had not yet discussed the matter with Princess Alexandra's parents (she was about to depart for Brussels to do just that), the Prince of Wales had only met the sixteen-year-old girl for a few minutes in Germany the previous year, while the possibility that the Princess might say "No" to a young man whom she knew had been sharing the bed of Nellie Clifden was a possibility to be considered. The Prince was due to visit Sandringham early in September to take a closer look at his new property. He did not arrive. He was bundled off to Ostend and Brussels to fix the engagement. He was somewhat sarcastic about the proceedings, commenting: "I hope everything will turn out to everybody's satisfaction."[6] So General Knollys and Mr White, the solicitor, travelled to Lynn alone.[7] Gerard talked with Mr White. He made it quite clear that, if Appleton was to become a game farm, he was withdrawing there and then. He asked for a special agreement that game should not be increased during the tenancy, adding that he was prepared to leave this to the honour of the landlord.

> He was assured that we need be under no apprehension, and the rent was fixed with the agreement that no injury should be done by ground game; and I believe Mr White meant what he said, for he had been one of the Prince Consort's men of business, and had he lived I feel sure he would have insisted upon the promise being carried out to the extent of his power. He seemed very anxious to secure my husband for the Appleton Farm and thought it would be nice for the Prince to have him there, and having informed us that it was the wish of our "illustrious landlord" that we should be "liberally treated", and inspected our banker's book and pronounced it to be quite satisfactory, we proceeded to invest the contents in all hope and confidence.[8]

Louise did not see her new home until the preliminary legal details had been settled, but she had learned something of it through enquiries amongst local farmers and tradesmen who had ventured there in the way of business. She learned that it "were a mucky hole" and "a downfally place, and not fit to live in". She learned, too, of the tenants, who were still in residence. They had made their pile in the days of cheap labour and war prices and, once a shilling was added to the pile, it stayed there. East Anglian farmers have long been known for a shrewdness with money which amounts to meanness, and here was a classic example. No brick that fell down was ever replaced, no fence or gate mended, no track repaired. It was take, take, take—from land, from animal, from tree. No money was spent on personal comfort, health or hygiene. Pounds had taken priority over God, nature and humanity. When the day came for Louise to set out on her first tour of inspection, she had formed a clear picture of what to expect, both of the place and of its occupants. "I was not prepared for much, but my imagination had not stretched to the scene of dirt, ruin and desolation."[9]

Their brougham lurched through the ruts and potholes of a track which, through years of neglect, had suffered an inverted process, being sunk in the middle and high at the sides. The horse struggled up a rise and splashed through a sea of slush to the main door. There stood two Uriah Heaps, hands clasped before them, wan smiles summoned up in welcome.

It was soon apparent that urgent instructions must have come from Sandringham regarding the inspection, for wine was laid out upon a table and a woman had been called in from the village to scrub the place out. Louise later learned that the old men had excused themselves for this unwarranted expense by saying that it was in compliment to the lady. But one woman with a brush and a pail could not displace the dirt of ages and Louise spotted the bugs which swarmed in clusters, while the rats, which ran at her coming, took refuge in the dairy milk leads.

The house was a maze of doors, none of which fitted and all of which creaked. There were nine separate entrances, so that one could walk straight outside from the majority of the ground-floor rooms. Upstairs there was no corridor, one room leading out of another. The windows were cracked and shrunken in their frames. The lower floors were of brick and in one dreary den, its window covered by creeper, a spring had forced its way up through the crevices.

The farm buildings defeated Louise's powers of description. If a waggon had collapsed through age and lack of care, there it lay. "The land was utterly exhausted and appeared to have been neither manured nor weeded for years, whilst broken gates and miles of rotten fencing completed the list of dilapidations."[10]

Louise made a further visit before moving in and it was then that she decided that the ground-floor rooms were not fit for habitation.

The damp and the draughts were an open invitation to fever and rheumatism. Accordingly she planned out the living accommodation through the upper floors, reserving the ground for storage. As soon as the old men had sneaked off into oblivion with their hoard, she hired local labour to wage war on the bugs and the rats.

The indoor servants at Sedgeford, unaware of the fate which lay in store for them, agreed to make the move to Appleton. The "backus boy" was left behind as one of his kind had been inherited from the old men. Bailiff Rumbles and his wife hummed and haahed, first said they would come and then said they would not, but eventually did. They were unwise, but their love for Louise was great. As there was no cottage for them, they set up home in a large shepherd's hut on wheels, which lay anchored like an ark in the sea of mud. Louise was convinced that one night the lads of the village would come with a horse and rope and tow them away into the night as they slept.

Despite Louise's cheerfulness, and the fires which she had lit in all the rooms to dry the place out, the staff from Sedgeford could not stomach Appleton. The lady's maid from London, looking at the rain falling on the dead rats on the muck-heap, realised that this was her Armageddon and speedily took train from Lynn. The cook announced that to stay would "injure her prospects" and followed suit. The younger ones saw no social future in either West Newton or Flitcham and returned to the land which they knew. Certain local women, accustomed to the isolation and the mud, took their place, assisted by an "antediluvian" who pottered about on odd jobs. In the case of the "backus boy", a rehabilitation course was necessary. One morning a dramatic, dismal yell echoed through the farm house. The boy had broken a plate while washing up. Accustomed as he was to "the dreadful old-fashioned floggings", he anticipated the arrival of the Cresswells suitably armed. Having been calmed at length, he explained that one of the former tenants, Master William, "did use to lay on to 'em"!

Isolated in the decayed parish of Appleton, where even the church was in ruins, Louise and Gerard felt cut off from the world. Their first outside task was to make their approach road passable for carriages and pedestrians. Their second was to improve communications. Mail arrived from Lynn on only two days of the week. Here certain family influence was used and shortly the postman was calling daily. And the arrival of a letter made a great difference to a day passed in that "downfally place".

SOURCES

1   Cresswell, p. 21
2   Ibid., p. 60
3   27th May 1865
4   Cresswell: *Norfolk and the Squires, Clergy*, etc., p. 19
5   *The Prince Consort*
6   Duff: *Victoria Travels*, p. 203
7   *Lynn Advertiser*, 6th September 1863
8   Cresswell, pp. 60–1
9   Ibid., p. 24
10   Ibid., p. 26

8

Royal Favour

The rains came. Louise uncovered an alpenstock which she had used on a holiday in Switzerland and prodded through the mud, jumping from one firm footing to the next. Gerard set about the serious business of farming. He estimated that it would take seven or eight years before he could get "heart" into the land again and that the cost would be high indeed. But he was young and took satisfaction from the knowledge that in the end he would have an excellent light land farm. He had no trouble with the steward at the Hall (as it was then known) since the position was held by one of the Brereton family, the family whose name has been twined in the story of Sandringham. Brereton was a "character" and of great interest to the newsmen who flocked to Norfolk to inspect the new home of the Prince of Wales. One thus described him:

> A steady, quiet, respectable man . . . but who has devoted himself all his life to a practical joke in the matter of dress. We suppose a genteel highwayman of the last century has furnished him with the pattern of his habiliments, which are familiar to all frequenters of Lynn market and other places of local resort. He is a fine, rather handsome man, with long black hair, curled in innumerable little ringlets which overhang his shoulders, a brigand's hat with conical top, embroidered coat, riding-whip, with breeches and boots to match. He generally appears in public with an *alter ego*, and, although custom takes off the droll effect where the pair are known, we fancy they would cause an amusing sensation in the Park or Regent Street.[1]*

Social callers there were in plenty, egged on by curiosity and the desire to obtain an early foothold on the royal estate. It was the arrival of the "carriage company" which Louise came to dread. The coachmen, accustomed to paying visits to grand houses and bowling up long drives, were defeated, geographically, by Apple-

* Mr Brereton died in 1874. His house was replaced by a "Folly".

ton. Invariably the route of approach that they chose was a low road, which to them appeared to have some resemblance to a drive. In the event it was a trap of pothole and quagmire and, from the hill, Louise would watch the inevitable catastrophe. The carriage would tipple to an alarming angle, the coachman hurry to the horses' heads, the footman jump from the box and open the door, and out into the ooze would step elderly aunts and gesticulating uncles and children decked out in their party clothes. By the time the steaming horses had been attended to, springs repaired and muddy guests refurbished, there was hardly time for a cup of tea before the party must depart—this time in the care of a pilot—to escape the snares of nightfall.

But if such visitors were hoping to catch a glimpse of Sandring-ham's new squire, they were to be disappointed, for his mother was still determined to keep him well out of the way. After travelling to Coburg to report to her on his engagement talk with Alexandra, Bertie had been despatched on a tour of southern Europe in the care of his elder sister and her husband, the Crown Prince and Princess of Prussia. He was therefore away from Eng-land both for his coming of age and the official announcement of his marriage.

Several reasons prompted the Queen to take this line of action. Playing for safety, she did not wish Bertie to become on intimate terms with Alexandra during the engagement period. The affair with Nellie Clifden was ever in her mind and she had just learned that her second son, Alfred, had likewise indulged,[2] leaving her in no doubt as to the sexual awareness of her offspring. Another reason was her "horror"[3] of the family of Princess Alexandra's mother, and she was determined to keep Bertie away from them. She said :

> The Prince of Wales is so weak that he would be sure to get entangled with Princess Louise's relations, and it would be *too* horrid if he should become one of *that* family.[4]

It was the Danish connection that had been the fear in the mind of the Prince Consort and he had expressed the view that the German influence must predominate. Thus the Prince of Wales was now instructed that he must write to his fiancée in German.[5] The Queen wrote to the Crown Princess : "I hope that you have 'germanised' Bertie as much as possible, for it is most necessary."[6]

A third reason was that Queen Victoria wished to prepare Alexandra for the life which lay ahead of her, and she was determined that there should be no outside influence during the inculcation period. Accordingly Alexandra was ordered to Osborne for three weeks of November. Her mother, from whom she had not previously been parted, was, most pointedly, not invited, and her father, Prince Christian, who brought her to England and later returned for her, was on neither occasion asked to be a guest at Osborne. He put up at a London hotel.[7] This was extraordinary, and bordering on bad manners, particularly since, at the time of the Queen's Coronation, he had been in the running to become her husband and she had showed him much favour.

Alexandra quickly won the heart of the Queen, who wrote to the Crown Princess:

> She is one of those sweet creatures who seem to come from the skies to help and bless poor mortals and brighten for a time their path![8]

Adjectivally, the girl was inundated—dear, gentle, good, simple, unspoilt, honest, straightforward, tender, affectionate, intelligent, cheerful, merry, and solid.[9] For her part, Alexandra learned to understand and respect her future mother-in-law, but in after years would break into her delightful chuckle as she told of the ordeal through which she had passed when she was "on approval".[10]

Albert Edward was allowed a short meeting with this treasure on her way back to Denmark and thereafter turned his attention to Norfolk. On a day shortly before Christmas, 1862, the sound of shooting came from the woods and heath of Sandringham. It was the Prince's first taste of the sport which was to dominate his life in Norfolk. He wrote to Mrs Bruce, widow of his former governor:

> Fancy on Saturday last a reporter from Lynn actually joined the beaters while we were shooting, but as I very nearly shot him in the legs as a rabbit was passing, he very soon gave me a wide berth. Gen. Knollys then informed him that his presence was not required, and he "skidaddled", as the Yankees call it....[11]

While the Prince had been sightseeing in the Mediterranean sunshine, Gerard and Louise had passed the long, dark evenings playing a game of dreams. Once the light went, they were isolated by the sea of mud and, huddled by the fire to escape the draughts, they would talk of the house and the buildings that they would put up if only that dream came true. They chose the site for a new house, sketched their plan of it, laid out the design for the dairy, the cowsheds, the stables. One day they had an unexpected visitor. It was the Queen's delightful old land-steward from Osborne, despatched by her on a visit of inspection. He was horrified at what he saw. Accustomed to the meticulous ways of the Prince Consort, the neat farm houses, the tiled and sterilised dairies, the ordered fields and fences, he returned south to make such vigorous representations to Her Majesty that orders were speedily given for the demolition of Appleton and all its appendages, and that in their place should rise a unit in keeping with the standards of Albert. No wonder that Louise was convinced that, if Albert had lived to the allotted span, the troubles which beset her would not have occurred. The land-steward had taken back with him the plans which Louise and Gerard had made before the fire, and they were informed that these plans would form the basis of the new farm.

A few weeks before his marriage in March 1863 the Prince of Wales rode up to Appleton to make the acquaintance of his tenants. Louise and Gerard were captivated by him. He was at his most charming and had, he said, heard all about them from Spencer Cowper and the steward at Osborne. In fact, Louise found difficulty in believing that he was really a Prince. He thought that Appleton was the queerest place and rocked with laughter as he raced upstairs and explored the rooms.

Louise next saw him at Easter when he introduced his wife to Sandringham.

> A characteristic reception was given them by the county gentry and peasantry, huntsmen gathering in their scarlet uniforms, while some 200 school children, strewing flowers and bearing flags, appeared to hail the Princess.[12]

She obtained a closer look at the bride on Easter day in the church of St Mary Magdalene. Dean Stanley took the service and gave the first English Sacrament to the girl whom he dubbed "this Angel in the Palace".[13] All Sandringham fell in love with the Princess on that morning, and none more deeply or sincerely than Louise Cresswell.

In the summer the rebuilding of Appleton began. It was only a small part of the vast construction programme which was to revolutionise Sandringham. Park House was built for General Knollys, houses went up for the head gardener and the head keeper, kennels arrived for the dogs and tiled stables for the Princess's ponies; £60,000 had been allowed by the Prince Consort in his original estimate of a suitable amount for improvement— Albert Edward spent £300,000.[14] His income simply could not stand it and thus he became prey to the money-lenders of Europe.[15] But this was no worry for Gerard and Louise and they watched, entranced, their new home rise from its foundations. They moved in as soon as it was habitable and they had no regrets as the "downfally" old farm house came tumbling down. From the up-stairs windows they could see, to one side, over their sweeping farm lands and the smart new buildings in keeping with a royal estate; and, to the other, over Sandringham heath and the cathedral-like pines which became a blaze of glory when the sun set into the sea behind them. There was one act of preservation to comply with. An old lady, who was one of the last of the Pastons, asked that relics of her family's residences there should be allowed to stand—"the old nut walk and entrances to under-ground passages, the ruined church and ancestral vault, the syca-more trees by the Pilgrims' Well, perhaps sown originally by those very pilgrims who made Appleton a halting place on their way to the celebrated shrine of Our Lady of Walsingham, guided there by the light of the Milky Way...."[16]

The Cresswell lamp shone brighter yet when an invitation arrived from T.R.H. to attend a dance in the drawing-room of the Hall.[17] Now they were both architecturally and socially sound.

SOURCES

1 *London Society*, Vol. II, 1862, p. 437
2 Fulford: *Dearest Mama*, p. 122
3 Magnus: *King Edward the Seventh*, p. 87
4 Ibid.
5 Fulford: *Dearest Mama*, p. 126
6 Magnus: *King Edward the Seventh*, p. 89
7 Ibid., p. 88
8 Fulford: *Dearest Mama*, p. 130
9 Ibid.
10 Magnus: *King Edward the Seventh*, p. 88
11 Lee: *King Edward VII*, Vol. I, p. 144
12 Paul: *Britain's King and Queen*, p. 139
13 Sanderson: *King Edward VII*, Vol. II, p. 19
14 Nicolson: *King George V*, p. 51
15 Magnus: *King Edward the Seventh*, p. 273
16 Cresswell, p. 31
17 Ibid., p. 164

9
The Shadow of the Gun

Hurrah! Hurrah! For our game preserves,
Hurrah for the fat battue,—
A flush of pheasants at every hedge,
And for each man loaders two! . . .
What property so stands in need
Of law's protecting arm,
As pheasants, hares and partridges
That do nobody harm,—
Save grumbling tenants who complain
That they won't let them farm?[1]

The railway line from King's Lynn to Wolferton was in operation by the autumn of 1863 and carriages were waiting at the royal station to transport the guests arriving for the twenty-second birthday of the Prince of Wales. This was the first of the birthday celebrations and shooting parties which were to continue until the last year in the life of King Edward VII. Tales filtered out of the gay goings-on at the Hall and fusillades came from the woods.

Now, when Gerard came home from the fields, he told of seeing strangers, men in German-type uniforms who, although civil, moved with authority about his land. They were the advance guard of the army of keepers which was to police the policies at Sandringham. They had been trained at Windsor, under the severe rules laid down by the Prince Consort. Albert had impressed his keepers "with a sense of the extreme importance of their work".[2] "Velveteens" were strange men, hard, lonely, always at war, not only with the vermin but also with the poachers. Power in their hands became corrupted, and they knew full well that the magistrates would take their word against that of all others. "A gamekeeper could easily swear away an enemy's liberty, and commit acts of brutality and oppression without punishment."[3] On two occasions the harshness of the Windsor keepers towards poachers and trespassers had been criticised in the House of Commons, and in both cases fines which had been imposed were paid by a Member.

Strangers were suspect and unwelcome in rural Norfolk, except for the "high ups" who were in a class apart and had the advantage of money in their pockets. For a man of one village to pay an evening visit to a public house in another was interpreted as an invitation to take part in a fight. These uniformed keepers upset the peace of mind of both the farmers and their workers. They appeared unexpectedly at all hours of the day and night, and their civility extended only to those whom they considered to be their superiors. One farmer thus complained about them to Louise:

> They're always a-spyin' here and a-pryin' there and a-watchin' everythink I du, and at my time o' life it ain't pleasant, and then the head-keeper he goo by and he niver touch his hat and look at me as much as to say "You're no friend o' mine." That's how *he* look; and then when I goo reound and see those Kangaroos (the hares) a-hoppin' and jumpin' about my crops, it make me right ill it du.[4]

The under-keepers patrolled the Appleton fields as if they were policemen on a beat. It was their job to rear as much game as the land would carry and they rendered regular reports to the head-keeper, detailing any obstacles in their way. The head-keeper would, if he considered it necessary, pass on these reports to the Prince. The Prince was not the kind of man to pause to consider the rights and wrongs of the case. Shooting had become "a perfect passion with him and nothing made him more angry than the slightest opposition to it".[5]

Worse was to follow. Without prior leave or consultation, men appeared on the Appleton land and began cutting strips across the fields until they looked like a gridiron. Trees and shrubs were planted to form game shelters and, until these grew to a sufficient height to smother them, weeds grew in wild profusion and the seeds blew through the crops and over the newly cleaned land. The Cresswells were not allowed to clear these weeds away, for fear of disturbing the birds nesting there.

High flying pheasants were then not in fashion and planting was done "without regard for the aerial course a bird would follow after being ejected from the covert's edge".[6] The Prince of Wales was, in fact, opposed to any design plan which would result in raising the flight path of the pheasants, for the very good reason that this would result in a smaller bag. The size of the bag was paramount. One of the "old school" who shot at Sandringham for many years, commented:

> The coverts which he planted were designed with no intention of producing pheasants which could possibly fly either high or fast . . . Dersingham Wood . . . consisted of a dense semicircular thicket of broom, snowberry, privets and the like, around which were planted at intervals wide screens of clipped evergreens about seven feet high. Behind these lurked complacently guns and loaders, some of them only just more mobile than the pheasants from which they were hidden.[7]

The game multiplied. Rabbits were bad enough, but at least they eat straight forward, clearing everything as they go, and could be controlled by fencing. It was the "kangaroos" which did the damage. The Cresswells wondered where they all came from, apparently being unaware of the Coburg custom of buying live hares in lots of a hundred.[8] They battered down the crops, breakfasted on the choicest of the swedes, and cut off the mangolds just as the saccharine juice was beginning to form in the joints. Sainfoin was gnawed down to the ground and the farm workers announced that it simply was not worth growing. They bit off the ears of the young wheat and raided the barley and the oats when they felt like a change of diet. Even the orchard and garden were not safe from them. The bark went from young fruit and rose trees, and not a crocus met the spring undamaged.

Once good sport could be ensured, the battues began. Preparations started at first light. The battlefield was cleared and the roads closed. The farm workers were ordered to take themselves and their machinery off the fields and thereafter to stay well out of sight in the farmyard. On one occasion the Cresswells had engaged a gang of thirty hands from a distance to "pull, top and tail, heap and mould up" turnips by the acre. For three days in succession the men were ordered off the land, whereat, quite understandably, they dispersed. Then frost set in and the crop was ruined. The Cresswells were not the only tenants to complain, but nothing was allowed to disturb the military precision of the slaughter.

> A complete silence having been secured for miles round, the day was ushered in by a procession of boys with blue and pink flags, like a Sunday School treat, a band of gamekeepers in green and gold, with the head man on horseback, an army of beaters in smocks and hats bound with Royal red, a caravan for the reception of the game, and a tailing off of loafers to see the fun, for H.R.H. is very

good-natured in allowing people to look on at his amusements, provided they do not interfere with them, and, if it could be conveniently managed, would perhaps have no objection to everybody's life being "skittles and beer" like his own.[9]

The grandson of the Prince of Wales, the Duke of Windsor, added sartorial detail to the scene:

> The gamekeepers wore bowler hats with gold cords round the base of the crown, and gold lace acorns on the front. But the head-keeper wore one of those half top hats, a "cheerer", and carried a silver horn—on a cord of red braid with tassels slung over his green, brass-buttoned coat of Melton cloth. The other keepers wore coats of green velveteen, introduced by the Prince Consort from Germany, with brass buttons, while their breeches were of tight cord, worn with gaiters. . . . The beaters used to wear smocks and black felt hats with blue and red ribbons, known as "chummies".[10]

Meantime the guests at the Hall had welcomed the day with tea and thin bread and butter, had been arrayed by their valets and stamped downstairs to the breakfast-room to make their choice from the vast selection of dishes available beneath the silver covers—kedgeree and kidneys, haddock and woodcock, bacon and poached eggs. Having filled themselves to capacity and made check of the sporting equipment necessary for the day, they paraded before the front door and prepared to mount.

Louise continues with the view from the tenant's eye:

> At about eleven o'clock the Royal party arrives in a string of waggonettes, and range themselves in a long line under the fences or behind the shelters put up for that purpose, each sportsman having loaders in attendance with an extra gun or guns to hand backwards and forwards, to load and reload. The boys and beaters are stationed in a semi-circle some distance off, and it is their place to beat up the birds and drive them to the fences, the waving flags frightening them from flying back. On they come in ever increasing numbers, until they burst in a cloud over the fence where the guns are concealed. This is the exciting moment, a terrific fusillade ensues, birds dropping down in all directions, wheeling about in confusion between the flags and the guns, the survivors gathering themselves together and escaping into the fields beyond. The shooters then retire to another line of fencing, making themselves comfortable with campstools and cigars until the birds are driven up as before, and so on through the day, only leaving off for luncheon in a tent brought down from Sandringham. . . .[11]

Yet Louise found this form of shooting superior to the real pheasant battue, "when the birds are brought up in hen-coops and turned out tame into the woods to be shot down in thousands". Much as she objected to the inroads that the hares made into their income, she was filled with disgust at the method of their slaughter. The "kangaroos" were in such number and so unaccustomed to being disturbed that they simply did not know how to care for themselves. They bobbed aimlessly about, some even sitting bolt upright in surprise. Louise commented that the "sportsmen" might as well have shot at sheep in a fold, and was only grateful that nobody suggested such a pastime, as H.R.H. might have included it in the programme.

The Cresswells dreaded the days devoted to partridge-driving, for it was then that the village boys made carnival. Knowing that they were under the protection of the Prince, they surged across the countryside, trampling down all that came before them, breaking down fences and gates and generally indulging in an orgy of mischief-making.

When the light began to fail, the battue was over and the guests drove back to prepare for festivities more in the feminine line, Gerard and Louise would ride out on their ponies to see the extent of the damage. Sad music was all around them—"the mournful chirruping of the poor little birds for their lost relatives".

Louise was later to realise that it was in these early days that a firm stand should have been taken at this blatant breach of the arrangement made with the Crown solicitor. But there were good reasons why she did not. Firstly, her husband's relations had made it very clear to her that they considered the Appleton tenancy to be Gerard's great chance and that she must not stand in his way. They would certainly not have considered a field of spoiled turnips sufficient cause to move on to a state of daggers drawn with the Heir to the Throne. She had made her views clear before leaving Sedgeford and knew full well that, if anything went wrong, it would be her fault. Secondly, having received a splendid new house, and buildings to match, it would appear like biting the hand that fed to curtail the Prince's amusement. Thirdly, she was deeply occupied with the nursery department.

Louise's first child, a daughter, was born on 10th April 1863, at the Bank House, King's Lynn,[12] the home of Gerard's mother. She was named Frances Dorothea after her great-grandmother.* The baby, whose health was a constant source of worry to Louise, lived for only nine months.

* Frances Dorothea Cresswell (1768–1832) married Francis Easterby, of Skinninggrove, Yorkshire. He purchased the other co-heir moiety of Cresswell and assumed the surname and arms of Cresswell in 1807.

January 15th 1864 . . . at the Bank House, the residence of her grandmother, Frances Dorothea, the only child of Gerard Oswin Cresswell, of Appleton, and Louise Mary, his wife. . . .[13]

Happiness came again when a son was born on 9th October of that year.[14] He was named Gerard after his father. A very good "nanny" now joined the household, a faithful treasure who held Louise's hand during all her troubles and stayed with her until she closed the door of Appleton for the last time. But, although Louise gained one friend, she lost another. Mrs Rumbles, the bailiff's wife, died during the winter. Louise had nursed her and missed her sadly when she had gone. It was she who had chased and chivvied and scolded the men on the farm, the servants and the "backus boy", and settled many a little problem which would otherwise have been laid before Gerard. But she had a heart of gold and the farm did not seem the same place without her. Mrs Rumbles had extracted a promise from Louise that she would find a "steady respectable person" to care for old Rumbles, and such a one, far beyond the age of romance, was installed in his kitchen. After a month's trial, the two were married. But the new Mrs Rumbles, excellent as she proved to be in cooking and caring for the cottage, showed no interest in agricultural matters, a lack which showed in the diminishing efficiency of the bailiff.

The summer of 1865 was dry and hot and the game population flourished. Gerard was one of those strong and cheerful men who made even the dullest room seem brighter when he entered it. But now, when he returned for meals, he was silent and had no appetite. In the evenings he would sit in his chair, lethargic, staring at nothing. When prompted into conversation, he would rant on endlessly about the destruction that was overtaking his crops, about the pheasants and partridges, rabbits and hares which covered his fields like a plague of locusts. He was worried about financial matters and weekly sank deeper and deeper into the slough of depression. Louise had decided that the time had come for a showdown over the increase in game. She knew that her husband, in full health, was fully capable of making the necessary remonstrances, and, if these failed, "waging open war". But, looking at him, she changed her mind, saying that they must put it off until the Prince came down.

Gerard came to a state of maniac depression. The damage being done to his farm haunted his days and sent nightmares through his sleeping hours. Louise always remembered:

I had many and bitter experiences in after years but I minded this more than all. I sometimes felt he might have recovered if this had not been laid upon him, adding to the natural depression of the illness which at last drifted into hopelessness.[15]

Gerard was suffering from "low" fever and the doctor shook his head when Louise asked if he would recover. She took him away for the last few weeks. It was essential that he be relieved from all cares and worries, and his former mentor, Mr Broome, took over the farm. He smiled at her, but the curtains were closing. Gerard Cresswell died on 27th October 1865 and was buried at North Runcton.[16] He was only twenty-eight.

SOURCES

1 Punch—on "*the Night Poaching Bill*", 26th July 1862
2 Jerrold: *Married Life of Queen Victoria*, p. 265
3 Ibid.
4 Cresswell, p. 65
5 Ibid., p. 62
6 Buxton: *The King in His Country*, p. 2
7 Ibid.
8 Duff: *Albert and Victoria*, p. 240
9 Cresswell, p. 69
10 Windsor: *A Family Album*, pp. 42–3
11 Cresswell, p. 70
12 *West Norfolk Gazette*, 18th April 1863
13 Ibid., 23rd January 1864
14 Ibid., 15th October 1864
15 Cresswell, p. 62
16 *Lynn Advertiser*, 4th November 1865

10

Alone

Alone. . . . Three years of marriage and three houses. . . . Two names on a gravestone in a quiet churchyard near King's Lynn.

Lost in the swirling mists which drift between life and death, earth and Heaven, weeping at the loneliness of each morning's waking, weak from the strain of watching her man die, Louise fought for sense and sanity. She ached for an opiate, some distraction which would fill every moment of the meaningless day, free from the bitter-sweet song of memory. For a time she planned to follow in the steps of Florence Nightingale and nurse in some big hospital. Then other sights and sounds prevailed.

In the nursery at Appleton a baby played and slept, a child too young to remember his father. From its stable Gerard's pony demanded exercise. His dogs looked up at her and pleaded for a walk around the fields. His men brought her urgent problems. The truth came to her that she could not break faith with the way of life which Gerard had built, that she must provide a home and a future for their son. The house was not to be let without the farm. Clearly she saw what she must do. She would turn farmeress and handle nine hundred acres and twelve hundred head of live stock on her own. People said that she was mad. They said that she was still young and should start afresh, that the wide world was open to her.

> It is all very well to be told the wide world is all before you; the wide world seemed to me to be a very dreary place and I shrank from going out into it.[1]

Despite the "croaking" of her friends, the farming folk around, who had held Gerard in high esteem, backed her in her decision, and none more strongly than Mr Broome. Gerard had whispered to Louise before he died that she must rely on Broome, and wise did his words prove, for this old friend undertook all the necessary legal arrangements relating to her becoming the tenant of Appleton. She thanked him and he replied that when the time came when he was no use to anybody, he was best under the sod. But one man objected strongly to Louise's chosen career and that was the Rev. Charles Kingsley, broad churchman, poet, novelist, author of *The Water Babies* and chaplain to Queen Victoria.

When the Prince of Wales joined Trinity College, Cambridge, in January 1861, the Prince Consort selected Kingsley, the newly appointed Professor of English History, to be his teacher. While at Oxford, Goldwin Smith had made little progress with Albert Edward, dismissing him as plain stupid. Kingsley adopted a more sympathetic line with considerable success. The two became firm friends and, after leaving Cambridge, the Prince appointed Kingsley his own Chaplain and he became a frequent week-end guest at Sandringham.[2] Although the gifted clergyman liked a day's hunting and was a good judge of a horse,[3] he could not tolerate his host's shooting activities. One day in Wolferton Wood, as "the merry brown hares" lay thick on the ground, limp, writhing, screaming, Kingsley marched up to the Prince and told him, straight to his face, how wrong it was.[4]

Kingsley's interests lay in other directions and he early discovered that the Cresswells shared his tastes. He would stride over from Sandringham, attired in Norfolk jacket and knickerbockers and puffing away at his pipe. He would ferret around Appleton for Roman, Danish, Saxon and Norman remains, talk of the story of stones,[5] and then, lying flat on the grass, observe the ways of beetles and caterpillars.[6]

Hearing of Gerard's death, Kingsley hurried over to Appleton, in the mixed rôles of man of God, friend and adviser. Louise saw him approaching. He was tall and spare, and that morning he looked more like a scarecrow than usual. He was an admixture of love and hot temper and there were signs of his restless, excitable temperament from far away.

> I can see him now . . . stammering more than ever from nervousness, using no hackneyed words of consolation, but so sorry for me, and hardly able to say anything but "My d-dear lady, p-pray don't, you'll r-ruin yourself". . . .[7]

He argued, using his own line, "Be good, sweet maid, and let who will be clever." He attempted to tell her, in his attractive stammer, of the catastrophe which had overtaken relations of his who had taken up farming. But he could make no impression on the calm determination of Louise and suddenly he turned, hardly waiting to say goodbye, and rushed away as if he could stand it no longer.

But he had brought a feeling of comfort and a sense of being wanted to a lonely and rather frightened widow.

Louise was to find many friends in the Sandringham orbit before her stay was out and, but for the influence of these friends, the Prince and his agent would have succeeded in having her out long before they did in fact manage to do so. They included the Rev. Lake Onslow, rector of the parish, whom she dubbed her "Knight and Champion"; George, Duke of Cambridge, ever ready to aid a pretty lady in distress; old General Hall, from Six Mile Bottom; Bernal Osborne, wit and connoisseur; Sir Anthony de Rothschild, a curious mixture of Hebrew financier and English country gentleman; and, not least, the Princess of Wales.

Mr Broome insisted that the first thing that Louise must do was to appoint a new steward. She knew full well that Mr Rumbles was long past his best, but she dreaded giving him notice as he was so proud and important in his new rôle of responsibility without the "Master". Each evening, when he came up for his orders for the morrow, the two would chat for a while of days gone by, of Mrs Rumbles on the trail of the "backus boy", of Gerard's skill with horses, of the "mean old men" of Appleton and the filth which they had left behind. At last she plucked up courage to tell him. He took it well, promised to show the new man his duties and said that he would always be around should the Mistress need him.

The new steward was named Dinger and he was young and smooth. He arrived with a sheaf of glowing references from Lords Lieutenant and the like, prompting Louise to wonder why they had parted with such a treasure. She put the question to him:

> He gave most satisfactory reasons for everything; some he had left from conscientious motives, and he would be quite overcome at the remembrance of what he had given up for righteousness' sake (never again will I believe in a man who talks about his conscience with the tears in his eyes). . . .[8]

For three months all went well and even Mr Broome was satisfied. Then the rot set in. Dinger was late at work in the mornings, forgot orders and stayed too long at the market. His relations began to die with tragic rapidity and in a "solemn suit of black" he would depart for their funerals. Word came to Louise that these funeral services were being held at a "skittle and beer" house in King's Lynn. She went to bed with an attack of influenza and, on recovery, was so horrified at the signs of neglect about the farm that she decided that Dinger must go. She summoned Mr Broome, who agreed with her, "blew up" the steward and gave him notice.

Now Dinger was the kind of man to whom words mean everything. He lived upon them, but despised those that he could fool with his verbiage. Most unexpectedly, he fooled the tough little Norfolk farmer. With those "eternal" tears in his eyes, he pleaded for his wife and children, thrown out without a roof to cover them. Mr Broome said that, if he behaved himself, he could stay until the end of the quarter. Dinger waited until a day or two before harvest and then announced that, unless he was given a rise in wages and a free hand with the harvest, he would leave at once. Louise told him that he could do just that and it was with relief that she watched him and his tiresome wife and children go.

But Dinger paid her out. He organised a rebellion among the harvest men and certain of them refused to begin cutting the corn until they received a considerable rise in pay. Louise was already paying as much as she could afford and accordingly told them to leave, without the option of changing their minds. But she was now in a dilemma over the "company" rule and the Norfolk labourer's refusal to stir out of the groove.

> They work at harvest times in what they call a "company" with a "lord" at the head. Each man is paid the same, part of which you give to the "lord" in weekly instalments and the balance at the end, and he keeps the account and divides it among them.[9]

Now the "company" was short in number and there was a shortage of labour in the area. Louise argued and pleaded, but the men would not start work until the "company" was at full strength.

> "They didn't see how it were to be done, they wouldn't a-minded one or two short, but the 'company' warn't nearly made up, and when the new chaps come in they mightn't like it, and things 'ud be onpleasant."[10]

Louise drove into Lynn and engaged several men who were waiting to be hired, but the majority of them who took her "shilling"—the sign that a bargain had been made—pocketed it and disappeared. Not daring to leave the farm again, she sent one of her trusted men to comb the public-houses and wharves, and "a pretty crew he returned with!" The police quickly arrived on the scene and took one of them away. Louise locked them up at night and let them out in the morning. She took over the job of steward and promoted her ploughman, a Methodist preacher, to foreman. The presence of religion among the men had a sobering effect and, except for some rowdiness as a result of too liberal indulgence in beer, the harvest went well. But, as Louise drove back alone from the bank in Lynn on pay nights, past the woods and heaths, she realised that she was a sitting target for Dinger or the rebels whom she had sacked.

Dinger did strike again, but only with his mouth. He demanded payment of wages up to the end of the quarter during which he was dismissed, Louise had paid him the proper amount due to him and took no notice. She then received a summons to appear at the County Court. Her solicitor told her that Dinger had engaged the most clever cross-examiner in East Anglia, Mr A. Hilker, and advised her to submit. But she was determined to do no such thing. She appeared in Court, backed by her eldest brother-in-law and co-executor, Francis Cresswell.

Hilker's opening peroration was so damning and fluent that Louise came to doubt whether she really was innocent. She watched the Judge making notes and was convinced that he believed every word. But when Dinger came into the box, she saw His Honour scanning him and felt a little hope. The steward was most convincing when answering his own counsel, but came to grief when cross-examined, particularly on the point of the identity of the corpses whose funerals he had attended. Mr Broome requested Hilker "to be so good as not to use such fine words", and won his round.

Poor Louise underwent three-quarters of an hour of hell in the box, constantly bombarded with statistical queries and points from her Labour and Wages books. She noticed that the Judge came to her rescue when she was sorely pressed. Returning to her seat, she was shown a note which had been passed from Hilker to her brother-in-law, in which her tormentor deplored the stern necessity that compelled him in the discharge of his professional duties to oppose anyone possessing the mental and personal attractions of "the fair defendant". Louise professed to be indignant but inside herself was complimented and delighted.

It remained only for her faithful shepherd, not just to deflate Dinger, whom he disliked, but also to convulse the Court with his down-to-earth remarks. Hilker elected to be "nonsuited with costs" and Dinger disappeared. It was a baptism of fire for Louise. She had stood firm and shown that she could win. Her next contestant was to be better armed and backed—none other than Albert Edward, Prince of Wales.

SOURCES

1   Cresswell, p. 33
2   Martin: *The Dust of Combat*, pp. 226–31; Lee: *King Edward VII*, Vol. I, p. 116
3   Cresswell, p. 148
4   Ibid., p. 146
5   Ibid., p. 31
6   Benson: *As We Were*, p. 10
7   Cresswell, p. 34
8   Ibid., p. 38
9   Ibid., p. 42
10 Ibid., p. 43

11

Battle Commences

"Kangaroos" everywhere.

When I rode or drove across the fields, they would start up at my pony's feet, gathering like a snowball, and run along before me like a little pack of hounds, while some of the most "owdacious" ones would stand upright on their hind legs with an air of irritating self-possession as if they knew they were Royal property and dared me to touch them. . . . Sometimes from curiosity to see the number there, I would give a "view haloo!" at the corner of a wheat field, when up would jump a swarm of little brown ears in the corn, like a regiment of soldiers in ambush.[1]

Louise tried every trick that she could think of to contain the flood, tarring the runs and stuffing the holes in the hedges with bundles of gorse. She saved one mangold crop by cutting up old canvas bags into strips, sewing them together and staking them round the field. She was told that she was making the place look as if she were taking in the washing of half Norfolk. She dare not take more drastic steps for fear of irritating the keepers into damaging her property at night.

Then she learned, through the rustic grape vine, that live hares were being imported, and that made her really angry. It was a blatant breach of the game arrangement. The news jolted the other tenant-farmers out of their usual rut of everlasting grumbling and they made an attempt at definite action. They staged quite a demonstration when attending the Audit and the oldest tenant on the estate gave notice to quit.

The Prince's London lawyer came down for these Audits and there met the county land-agent. Owing to Louise's preoccupation with the farm and her deep mourning for her husband, Mr Broome deputised for her and attended the rent dinner. But she realised that the time had come when she must speak for herself.

She was prompted to do so, not only by the hares, but also by the consideration of "vulgar money". She had been forced to borrow from the bank to pay the rent and there was no sign of payment by the landlord for the damage done to her crops by the game. In addition she had to pay five per cent interest on most of the cost of the house and buildings and was charged £300 for the carting of the materials. The place was left in an unfinished state, the builders being required for another of the Prince's enterprises, and she received word from H.R.H. that the tidying up should be done at once as he liked to see things in apple pie order when he came on tours of inspection with his friends. The high-handed treatment was degrading and for the first time in her life Louise felt that she was losing her pride, her confidence and her belief in herself. This she would not allow.

At headquarters, Sandringham, the point that Louise had to make a living was never accepted. It was a most convenient stand for Albert Edward and one that he often adopted. He would mercilessly strain the finances of others until they were bankrupt. So Louise was accused of being stubborn, awkward, and selfish in her efforts to curtail the pleasures of the Prince whose sole object was to improve the lot of the people around Sandringham. The headquarters' view was simply that, being a "lady", she should be "above" complaining or asking to be paid. When she requested a written acknowledgment of a certain farming agreement, she was met with raised eyebrows. Was she really doubting the word and honour of the Heir to the Throne? There were dark hints that if she wished to go upon a commercial footing, she would find that it was a great mistake.

It was often stated in print, and widely believed, that the Prince ran Sandringham himself, that if anyone had a complaint he received them personally, made enquiries and redressed grievances. He was thus held up as an example which other landlords should follow. Louise did not agree.

> During my long residence on the property, I never heard of the Prince receiving or listening to any of the residents on business matters. He seemed to hear all that was going on, too often in an upside down fashion, and all the news and gossip into the bargain; but I have often heard it regretted that it was impossible to tell the Prince how things stood. Kings may love those who speak the truth, but I suspect they very seldom have that felicity. I tried once or twice to put in a little wedge of business when honoured with the opportunity of conversing with his Royal Highness, but he was quite unapproachable upon estate matters; and as "manners are manners", I could not, when invited to his house, or when the

Royalties came to Appleton, intrude subjects upon him that he did
not choose to hear.[2]

Nor was the Comptroller of the Household, General Knollys,
delightful as he was, of much assistance, as he was away from
Norfolk for long periods at a time and was deeply involved with
his multifarious duties. Therefore approach had to be made from
a lower level, and there the old order was changing. The Prince
Consort's "legal man of business" had died and been succeeded
by his son, who lacked experience. And there was a new agent for
the estate, Edmund Beck, a sharp country auctioneer who had
been employed in selling wood in the plantations.

When the day for the Audit came round, Louise drove into
Lynn. The Meeting was to be held at an hotel, but she called first
at the Bank House to collect male reinforcements in the persons
of Frank, her brother-in-law, and an executor of Gerard's will. She
did not venture into battle unarmed, for she carried in her hand
a "bouquet" of mangold tops which the hares had bitten off. The
sight of the "bouquet" spread alarm and despondency in the hearts
of her relatives and was the signal for an outpouring of masculine
arguments of a pacifistic nature. "Come, Louise, you *can't* go with
that thing; it looks exactly like a bludgeon. I declare if you do,
I won't go; you'd much better not, it will only make a row."[3]

But there was no mercy for them in the heart of Louise and
she bundled them out of the door and marched them, "a couple
of victims", down the street to the hotel. There Mr Broome was
waiting. Up went his eyebrows when he saw the "bouquet" and
he put on his comical look, commenting that "it was not a bad
idea". As the four of them were ushered into the room reserved
for the Audit, the solicitor from London rose and "bowed down
to his toes". His manners were superb and compliments gushed
from him, but Louise guessed that there were claws in his velvet
gloves. Only she and he counted. The agent appeared nervous
and confused and hurried about the room pushing chairs under
people. Frank refused to sit, taking up station behind his sister-
in-law's chair. His face was clouded with funereal gloom. Some-
body made a damned silly remark about the weather. Then there
was silence. Each man there was waiting for the volcano that was
Louise to explode.

She let some seconds of suspense pass and then, smiling sweetly
at the solicitor, she placed the mangold tops on the table and said:
"I do not know where the rent is to come from, for my wheat is
cut to pieces and here is a specimen of the mangold crop."[4]

This unexpected opening somewhat deflated the sauve legal gentleman. He hurriedly explained that he was a townsman and knew little of the growth cycle of mangolds or the eating habits of hares. He looked, Louise thought, like a lodging-house landlady protesting that "a certain noxious insect was never seen upon her premises until you came along and invented it". Fortunately she had the backing of three men who knew all about such things and, after much parleying on their part, it was agreed that she should be paid for the damage done that summer. This was a great concession, as it was an admission that damage had been done and that there was a right to payment.

Mr Broome then made the point that the rent should not be paid until the amount of the game bill had been settled. Louise agreed. The opposition did not. At this point her remaining male support, relieved beyond measure at the peaceful outcome of the confrontation, showed signs of weakness. Louise heard Frank whisper, from behind her chair, "It will be all right, Louise, all right." The lawyer heard him also and quickly took the chance to close the meeting. He rose and bowed them out, "the obsequious land-agent opening the door for us and looking as if the door handle was his very best friend".

The lawyer and Mr Beck were now in a very difficult position. They were caught between two fires. Firstly, they had been instructed from above that any agreement as to damages must be kept secret and on no account must it reach the press. Albert Edward was unpopular at the time. "A whispering campaign about aspects of the Prince's private life ran through some sections of the community and found expression in *The Times* and other newspapers."[5] There was gossip about Hortense Schneider, of his betting and gambling and of his adventures while on the Continent. He was still the naughty boy who had been such a trouble to his parents, and many years were to pass before he was promoted to the "pantomime" Prince for whom all could be forgiven.

For the present the propaganda machine for the Sunday schools, ably abetted by Queen Victoria, was still working full blast on the deification of Albert. The Prince's advisers knew full well that if an enterprising reporter got his hands on the story of the martyrdom of a young widow and her son at Sandringham, untold harm might be done.

Secondly came finance. The Prince was "in the red" annually to the extent of some £20,000. He had paid too much for Sandringham and was spending too much upon it. Without the Norfolk investment, his account could have been balanced.[6] It was therefore vital that the figure for the rent return should be as high as possible. The agent, new to his job, was anxious to make a good impression by harvesting "a large haul of rentals". The Prince would certainly not look with favour upon a considerable sum being paid out to Mrs Cresswell.

The valuers assessed the damage done at Appleton farm to be as follows:

	£	s.
On 37 acres of wheat, average done 2 cmbs. per acre, at 20s. the cmb.	103	12
On 73 acres wheat, 1 cmb. per acre at 28s.	102	4
On 170 acres wheat, 1 cmb. per acre at 20s.	170	
On rye (25 acres), 6 bushels per acre, at 4s.	30	
Mangolds, damage on 24 acres, 50s. per acre	60	
Clover layers	50	
Turnips	60	
	£575	16[7]

Louise considered that this figure was far below the true value, but then she would have been unfaithful to the creed of her calling if she had thought otherwise. But to the Sandringham authorities it was much too high, and there were obvious signs of regret that they had agreed to paying any damages at all.

The stratagem adopted was to pay into Louise's bank account, without her knowledge, half the amount due, and a receipt for the payment of damages was obtained. Furious, Louise was all for sending back the amount paid in, but her financial advisers wisely reminded her that, should she do that, she might get nothing at all. They suggested that she sent a receipt marked "on account" and claim the balance. No result. In and in went the claims and, when there was added to them a hint of legal proceedings, the debt was at long last admitted. With the admission came the promise that payment would be made. But it never was. Louise commented:

> Verily if the word "goose" did not exist in the English language, it would have been invented on purpose for me![8]

SOURCES

1   Cresswell, p. 66
2   Ibid., p. 78

3 Ibid., p. 79
4 Ibid., p. 80
5 Magnus : *King Edward the Seventh*, p. 132
6 Ibid., p. 121
7 Cresswell, p. 82
8 Ibid., p. 84

12

Sensation in Parliament

Louise moved from the parochial level to the national. It was not her intention to do so. In her tenacious efforts to obtain the remainder of the damages due to her, she overlooked the point that her debtor was Heir to the Throne and that everything about him was "news". She was therefore somewhat unwise and over-trusting in confiding her troubles to a Member of Parliament.

Clare Sewell Read was Member for East Norfolk from 1865–68, for South Norfolk 1868–80 and for West Norfolk 1884–5. In 1875–6 he was Parliamentary Secretary of the Local Government Board in Disraeli's administration. He was an expert on agricultural matters, a firm friend of the farmers and frequently spoke on their behalf. He was an unassuming man and in the House thus proclaimed himself—"I, as a tenant farmer . . .", "I as a middle-class man. . . ." The "County" folk of Norfolk looked down their noses when he first became a candidate, but he more than held his own and all came to admire him.[1] Louise liked and trusted him. Therefore it was to him that she wrote, confiding her troubles.

In the rush of Westminster business, a misunderstanding occurred and Mr Read did not appreciate that Louise was but seeking his expert and confidential advice. Accordingly he stood up in the House and read out to the assembled Members the full text of her letter, which included particulars of the damages and non-payment of costs.

Louise sat down to breakfast at Appleton farm, picked up the paper and there read her own words which the day before had echoed throughout the House of Commons. She was both devastated and startled.

To think that after all their precautions the murder was out and through *me*![2]

In Marlborough House, London, another breakfast was simultaneously upset, that of H.R.H. the Prince of Wales. The Queen was at Balmoral. She had already requested her son to stop excessive preservation of game.[3] Now she sent for him—alone. It is readily understandable that Louise was correct when she wrote that thereafter,

> he scowled at me in true Henry the Eighth style whenever he chanced to meet me; and if Kings had power of life and death in these days, which I am glad they have not, I know where my head would have been. . . .[4]

The affair became the talk of the neighbourhood and, although opinions were sharply divided, few were prepared to back Louise openly as this would have entailed direct confrontation with H.R.H. But there were many people in Norfolk eager to climb on the royal band-waggon and prepared to give lip service to the Prince in the hope of receiving invitations to festivities at Sandringham. Louise was a man's woman—she was too efficient and outspoken for the liking of the majority of society ladies. She was also attractive and thus, when she slipped from grace, was due for the same treatment as was meted out to pretty girls in India who received more than their fair share of attention from the officers.

A business appointment called her to London and she took train from King's Lynn. She shared a compartment with some austere women who, having thrown her dark and searching looks, began whispering together. Thereafter, and throughout the journey, they talked between themselves, in the third person, of "she" who had persecuted the Prince of Wales and worried the poor Princess at a time when she was ill and concerned about her babies, of "she" who had been ungrateful for favours shown, etc., etc. Poor Louise shrank into her corner, gazing out at the countryside and wishing that Albert of Coburg had stayed in his German Duchy.

> For three long years I lived in an atmosphere of misrepresentation, black-lettered, labelled dangerous, looked upon suspiciously by courtiers from within and without, to the great concern of my good friend, Mr Onslow, Rector of Sandringham and Domestic Chaplain to their Royal Highnesses, who was distressed to see me in such a position, yet courageous enough (as he always was) where justice and fair play were concerned, to remonstrate with H.R.H. on my behalf, though without effect. My offence was beyond forgiveness, and the punishment might have gone on into perpetuity had not an event occurred that brought about an unexpected change for the better.[5]

In the summer of 1869 Louise was asked by Mr Beck if she would bring up a litter of fox cubs. She was somewhat surprised at being requested to do a favour while she was in such deep disgrace, but realised the reason behind it. Her brother had been a Master of Foxhounds in the Shires and, while working with him, she had learned the tricks of bringing up such litters. This was but one more chore in a busy life, but she agreed in the hope that it might augur the beginnings of a way back to peace. The cubs proved a great deal of trouble to contain, burrowing under the walls of their shed, and Louise was mightily relieved when she was directed to turn them into a brick earth at the end of her farm. She received a letter full of thanks for the trouble that she had taken.

The Prince was keen on hunting as a young man but when he was thirty informed his mother that he preferred "staghounds to foxhounds".[6] The Princess adored hunting, or rather the riding side, as she admitted that she "hoped the poor fox would get away".[7] The Queen tried to stop her so doing. She yielded for a while and then was back in the saddle.[8] When out with the West Norfolk she was a magnet which drew a field of five hundred and roads choked with carriages.

Having experienced a poor day with the West Norfolk around Snettisham, the Prince invited the master to try Sandringham, where he promised there would be fine sport. But not a fox broke from the Sandringham woods. This was just the kind of failure which irritated Albert Edward. If he said that there were foxes, foxes there would be. But there were no foxes at Sandringham because the keepers did not want them there. To prevent them "playing the deuce with the pheasants" fires had to be lit and men kept on patrol all night. Thus the game-preservers had little enthusiasm for hunting.

Sandringham was being rebuilt and was not yet ready for habitation, so at the end of 1869 the Prince rented Gunton Hall, Lord Suffield's place near Cromer,[9] and moved in with his family. Assured that she would not meet the spectre of Henry VIII in the living form of Albert Edward in Sandringham park, one afternoon Louise called at the Rectory. She was always welcome there.

Mrs Onslow said that her son, who had been shooting with the Prince at Gunton, would like a word with her. He would be in soon and would she please wait. Louise relaxed and enjoyed the Rectory tea. As soon as young Mr Onslow came into the room, she noticed that he was in a state of nerves and general agitation. Standing before the fire, shifting from foot to foot, he asked her if she had heard that seventy-one pheasants had been killed in the Sandringham plantations. Louise replied that she had heard something from her men about a number being missed in the woods one night.

Mr Onslow, now more nervous than before, continued: "But I am afraid that your name is mixed up with it in rather an unpleasant manner!"

"My name! What can I have to do with it?"

He looked down into the fire, unable to meet her eyes. Then the truth came to her, as stinging as a sudden slap across the face. She screamed across the cosy, lamp-lit room:

"You don't mean to say that they say I killed those pheasants?"

Mr Onslow replied that "Such was the case".[10]

As the Rector's wife plied soothing tea, the story came out.

The Prince had been entertaining a large party after a day's shooting. Among his guests were the Duke of Cambridge, old General Hall and young Onslow. A footman announced that the head gamekeeper from Sandringham had arrived and wished to speak to H.R.H. urgently. The Prince said: "Show him in." In marched the keeper and announced, before the assembled guests, that seventy-one pheasants had been killed by Mrs Cresswell in the Sandringham plantations.

There was an explosion. The Prince "blew his top". Later Louise was to hear from those who were there that they had never heard such a row in their lives. As the row waged and the men of the gun discussed the heinous offence, young Onslow drew General Hall on one side. The two knew Louise better than anyone else present. They were fully aware that she would not have done such a thing. Then, with a courage worthy of the Victoria Cross, they marched together into the cannon's mouth and respectfully requested that the lady in question be allowed the chance of defending herself. They volunteered to report the charge to Louise. But the Prince would not hear of it. He was always the same— if he heard a charge or accusation, he immediately accepted it as fact. Then one or two of the other guests volunteered that that was the only fair course. The balance was tilted by the Duke of Cambridge.

The Queen employed her cousin George as a channel of communication between herself and Sandringham. She would fill him with the sternest instructions and reprimands for delivery at the establishment described by a friend of Lord Clarendon's as "not at all a nice young Court",[11] but by the time that the Commander-in-Chief had reached Norfolk, his courage had waned and Vic-

1 Louisa (or Louise) Cresswell, *circa* 1864 *(from a photograph in the possession of Lady Harrod)*

11 Gerard Oswin Cresswell, Louise's husband, *circa* 1864 *(from a photograph in the possession of Lady Harrod)*

Above, III Portrait of the children of Francis Cresswell and his wife, Rachel Fry *(from a photograph in the possession of Lady Harrod)*; *right*, IV The Prince and Princess of Wales with their first child, Prince Albert Victor, in 1864 *(from the author's collection)*

Above, V Appleton Hall, Norfolk, *circa 1896 (from the author's collection); below*, VI Sandringham House as it was when the Prince of Wales took it over *(from the author's collection)*

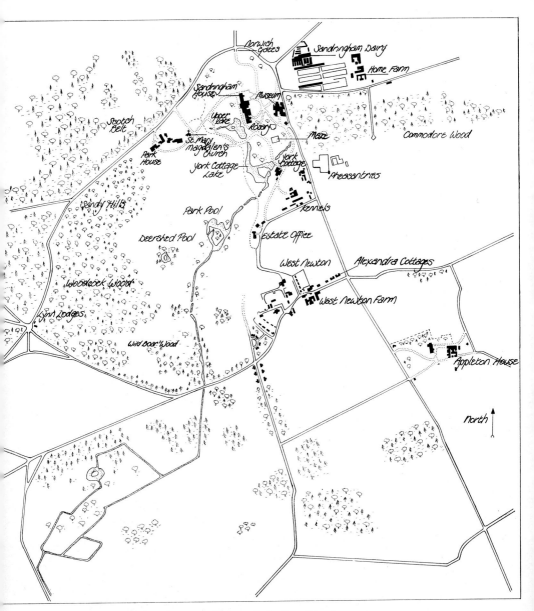

VII Sketch map of part of the Sandringham estate

VIII Edward and Alexandra on their wedding day, March 10th,
1863 *(from the author's collection)*

IX Sedgeford Hall as it was in 1950 *(by courtesy of Mr Bernard Campbell)*

Right, X The Prince of Wales rests during a day's shooting *(from the author's collection); below*, XI Edward has bagged one of the herd of wild bulls in the park of Chillingham Castle, Northumberland, 1876. The beast's head was later hung in the entrance hall at Sandringham *(from the author's collection)*

XII Christmas doles at Sandringham, from a drawing by Charles Sheldon.
The widow's garments of the woman in the left foreground would suggest
that she was in fact Louise Cresswell *(from the author's collection)*

XIII Sandringham Church as it was in the 1860s *(from the author's collection)*

XIV A rare etching of Edward and Alexandra *en famille (from the author's collection)*

XV The Prince of Wales in 1870 *(from the author's collection)*

Above, XVI Appleton House on the Sandringham estate: a modern photograph *(from the author's collection)*; *below,* XVII The interior of the Appleton Farm cowhouse as it is today *(by courtesy of the* Eastern Daily Press*)*

toria's edicts were much watered down before they were poured out to the Prince and Princess. The Duke was a ladies' man and had a soft spot for Louise. She liked him and enjoyed his sociable, George III habit of asking questions and then saying "What?", just as his father had done. She liked him more than ever after this day's business. Accustomed as he was to courts-martial, he now gave his decided opinion "that there should be an enquiry". And that, coming from the Commander-in-Chief, decided the matter.

The Prince, finding himself overruled, grudgingly agreed that Louise should be acquainted with the charge against her before being nailed to the cross. Mr Onslow was instructed to cross-examine her and then send a full, written report to General Hall. Louise's first reaction to the dictatorial approach was to "cut up rusty", say nothing, and let the Prince do his worst. She decided to co-operate in view of the trouble which had been taken by the Duke, the General and Mr Onslow to defend her.

She had by this time formed a shrewd idea of what had happened. She knew that the cubs would not leave a gorse covert swarming with rabbits and make their way into the Sandring-ham plantations. They were too young for such an adventure. She guessed that the culprit was a wily old dog-fox from Anmer, to the east. One of the men on night watch must have been caught off guard, with disastrous result. The man, unaware of the true position and anxious to cover himself, reported to the head keeper that Mrs Cresswell had turned loose her foxes. The head keeper, an irascible man, accepted the story without question and passed it on to the Prince.

Louise gave Mr Onslow a detailed account of everything that had taken place since the day when she was asked to care for the cubs, adding her theories as to what had happened. Mr Onslow wrote out his report and despatched it to General Hall. The General considered that it vindicated Louise completely and sent her a warm letter of congratulation.

By this time the Wales family had returned to Marlborough House and young Onslow, adding a bar to the medal which he had already earned, volunteered to take the report up to the Prince. This was no easy task, as H.R.H. was still in a flaming temper and, according to letters which Louise received from friends, spreading an embellished version of the decimation of his pheasants round the dinner tables of London. But a few days later the Rector arrived at Appleton with the news that the Prince was "more tempered now".

D   97

The final inquiry, held at Sandringham, was in the nature of a grand court-martial. H.R.H. attended. The Lord Lieutenant of the county, the Earl of Leicester, was in charge, undertaking the rôles of cross-examiner and umpire. Young Mr Onslow represented the interests of Louise. The head keeper and the agent gave their versions of what had happened. Eye-witnesses gave evidence regarding the rearing of the cubs and the damage done in the plantations.

> The evidence in my favour was so overwhelming that a verdict of "Not Guilty" was speedily arrived at, his Lordship being so good as to supplement it by placing my conduct and the difficulties of my position in the most favourable light to His Royal Highness, who graciously condescended to express himself satisfied with the result. . . .[12]

Just as Victoria's strange son was quick to blame, so also was he quick to forgive—or at least give a very good imitation of forgiveness. He sent an emissary to Appleton with the message that the whole affair had been due to a "misconception". When he met Louise about the estate, the smile of Bonnie Prince Charlie took the place of the scowl of Henry VIII. His friends and courtiers, who had previously looked at her as if she was "a species of Guy Fawkes in petticoats", now greeted her with gay acclaim. The next few years were to prove the most peaceful and properous of her stay at Sandringham.

Yet the battle had been too fierce, the accusations to acrid, for the bitterness engendered to dissolve in one forgiving smile. Reputations had been damaged and wounds festered. It was the head keeper who considered that he had been most hardly done by. He blamed the agent, for letting him down and not keeping him in the picture regarding the cubs.

Now the keeper was a large and pugnacious man and he thirsted for the blood of the agent. So fierce were the threats that Mr Beck did not dare risk a confrontation. Sandringham had had enough of notoriety and accordingly the keeper was transferred to a similar post at Windsor, where he became a close friend of the Queen's ghillie and personal servant, John Brown. In his place came Mr Jackson, a kind and reasonable man who stayed long and came to be numbered among the personal friends of the future King George V.[13]

SOURCES

1   Cresswell: *Norfolk and the Squires, etc.,* p. 27
2   Cresswell, p. 85
3   Magnus: *King Edward the Seventh,* p. 124
4   Cresswell, p. 86
5   Ibid., p. 87
6   Magnus: *King Edward the Seventh,* p. 124
7   Cathcart: *Sandringham,* p. 77
8   Battiscombe: *Queen Alexandra,* p. 73
9   Sanderson: *King Edward VII,* Vol. II, p. 145
10 Cresswell, pp. 87–8
11 Bolitho: *Victoria, the Widow and Her Son,* p. 41
12 Cresswell, p. 93
13 Gore: *King George V,* p. 364

13
A Miracle at Sandringham

The years 1870 and 1871 were exciting and dramatic on both the parochial and national levels. The first big event for the people of Sandringham was the building of the new house, dubbed "the Big House" to distinguish it from Park House and Batchelors' Cottage. In April the Prince escorted his wife over the threshold and inspected progress. He was far from pleased. Over the porch had been inscribed the words, "This house was built by Albert Edward and Alexandra his wife in the year of our Lord 1870", but he was in doubt whether this promise would be fulfilled. He demanded speed and more speed and, when he came back in September and found heaps of rubble and unfinished ceilings, he threatened that he would cancel the customary labourers' dinner held on his birthday, 9th November, if the house was not finished by then. It was.[1]

It had been a bad year for the Prince. In March he had been subpoenaed to appear in the divorce suit brought by Sir Charles Mordaunt against his wife, and twelve of his letters to Lady Mordaunt were read out in court. Thereafter he was hissed in the streets of London, at the races and at the theatre. His mother described the affair as "painful and lowering".[2] Then, in July, France marched against Germany. Cavalry trotting in the Parisian sunshine . . . uniforms of sky-blue, scarlet and green . . . clanking swords and flashing breast-plates . . . the crowds shouting "À Berlin!" . . . the last glory of the Second Empire. By the first week in September Napoleon III had been defeated and surrendered. Empress Eugénie and the Prince Imperial fled to England and the Republic was declared. Queen Victoria backed Germany—her people, France. The spirit of the new France crossed the Channel. On 19th September, at a crowded meeting in Trafalgar Square,

caps of liberty were hoisted on poles and the "Republic of England" proclaimed.[3] At a Republican meeting in October the Royal
Family was described as "a pack of Germans".[4] There were some
very nasty little rhymes in circulation about the Prince of Wales,
but on his birthday morning he received one of a very different
nature. It was a gift from his elder son, "Eddy", and read:

> *Day of pleasure*
> *Brightly dawning,*
> *Take the gift*
> *On this sweet morning:*
> *Our best hopes*
> *And wishes blending,*
> *Must yield joy*
> *That's never ending.*[5]

The spell of Sandringham was now firm upon Albert Edward.
Here, among his children, his guns, his dogs and horses, his model
villages, he found a peace which contrasted strongly with the
acrimony and pace which made up his life in London. De-training
at Wolferton, he became a man transformed. It was said of him:
"It would be as the breath of Heaven if the air of Sandringham
could be brought to Marlborough House."[6] Here, as squire, he was
determined to be popular and, although there were still those in
Norfolk who, looking towards the Princess, would remark, "It
is she who keeps the Throne for him", he was fast gaining his
way. For those who were implacably against him there was
always the alternative—out. To consolidate his position he decided
upon a series of house-warming festivities to celebrate the resurrection of Sandringham. Louise Cresswell received an invitation to a
ball to be held on 2nd December.[7]

She decided not to go. She had not been a guest of the Prince
since the drawing-room dance which she had attended with her
husband. In the interim period mourning, and then deep disgrace,
had put an end to further invitations. Isolated at Appleton, she
had forgotten what it felt like to go out in the evening. She was
not sure that she wished to sample the taste again. She had spent
so long, all day of every day, in a serge dress and thick boots
that the thought of the dance floor frightened her. Anyway she
was out of touch with fashion and had no idea what the modern
miss was wearing. She was not even sure that she was capable of
dressing herself—in her gay days there had always been a lady's
maid. But at the same time she was consumed with curiosity to
see new Sandringham House, who were the guests at the ball and

what they were wearing, so she took the coward's way out and decided to watch proceedings from the anonymity of the gallery.

She discussed the question with the Onslows. The Rector and his wife were horrified. If she did not attend as invited, it would appear as a slight to H.R.H. and as if she still resented the troubles which now were over. It was in her interest to go—she must go. "But the Prince would never notice if I was there or not!" pleaded Louise. There the Rector put her right—the Prince noticed everything about people, where they went, their birthdays, their ages and even their weights. He could check with one quick glance round the Church if any one of his employees, however junior, was playing truant. The Rector knew full well what would happen. The morning after the ball he would be summoned by the Prince and thus addressed: "Now then, Onslow, so your friend, Mrs Cresswell, did not choose to come, eh?" And what excuse could he give?

Louise had no choice but to change her mind. The immediate problem was to find something to wear. She fingered her way through drawers and cases and wardrobes, disturbing memories which had laid dormant since Gerard died. She decided on a trousseau gown which she had not worn since the Sedgeford days. She found some old lace which would smarten it up. She parcelled them together and sent them off to London for renovation and conversion to the 1870 style. She had made up her mind that, now that she had to go, she at least would not look a frump. She sought the confidence of the knowledge that she was well dressed—"that inward peace and composure that the godless Parisians say even religion cannot bestow".

On the morning of the ball Louise received a note from the Hon. Spencer Cowper, staying with the Prince for the first time since he had sold Sandringham. He said that he was looking forward to dancing with her. So there was to be one important partner.

That evening there was a maternal crisis in the cowshed. She was late going upstairs to change. Difficulty after difficulty arose during the delicate task of transfiguration from the farm girl to the belle of the ball. All her fingers were fat thumbs and she prayed for the quick hands of her erstwhile lady's maid. And in her rush and agitation she forgot one vital point—that the Prince always kept his clocks half an hour fast—"Sandringham time" it was called. She was therefore long behind schedule when, dressed at last, she reached the farm door.

It would have been nice if there had been a footman there, to open a carriage door and tuck a rug around her, a coachman on the box. But that was not for Louise. She came out into a lonely night, took up the reins of her trap and drove off alone through the black of the drive towards the lights and the sounds of Sandringham.

Only a mile to go, but a mile seemed longer then. The flickering candle-light from the carriage lamps faded out at the pony's head. Past the West Newton turn and along the park-side. Young trees stood sentinel beside the road, like soldiers lining the route, their thin shadows making steps along the way. Then the dark mass of Commodore Wood loomed up and she turned into the grounds of "the Big House".

Into a new world. The gas lights turned night into day. A groom took the reins. A footman helped her down. Maids took her cloak and magic hands put the ravages of the breeze to rights. It was then that Louise saw a clock and realised how late she was.

Meantime, inside Sandringham, there had been some consternation as to the whereabouts of the missing tenant-farmer. Before the dancing began, there was a reception, to make sure that all the three hundred guests had the chance to meet their host and hostess. The two stood under the brilliant candelabra as the queue filed in. The Princess was the star—it was her birthday ball.[8]* She was pregnant but lovely as ever. The Rector and Mrs Onslow, as their standing demanded, were early on the scene and keeping close watch for Louise. The long queue passed and thinned, but still no sign of her. The Prince enquired as to whether Mrs Cresswell was coming and was assured that she was and that her gown had come from London. Now he too was watching the door. The Onslows fretted and fussed, fearing that some crisis had overtaken Appleton farm or that Louise was lying by the roadside with the trap on top of her.

The proceedings could no longer be delayed and Coot and Tinneys band struck up from the gallery. The Prince and Princess took their places for the Royal Quadrille. This was the customary opening for the Sandringham balls, T.R.H. dancing with the guests of highest rank. The dainty dance was well under way when Louise, ashamed of herself, slipped into the ballroom, praying that her absence had not been noted. The Prince spotted her immediately. Leaving the second senior lady in the room to cope as best she could without a partner, he hurried across to Louise, greeted her with obvious delight and shook hands with her, an *amende honourable* which she deeply appreciated. Suddenly she was ten feet tall.

* Born 1st December 1844.

All the worries and sadnesses of the past seven years faded away as if they had never been. The spell of the music, the moving tapestry of silks and tulles and diamonds, the brilliant setting of the new house, the welcome of old friends and the compliments of partners, brought to her a haze of happiness which enriched her loveliness. Happiness was a drug which reacted strongly because there had been so little happiness and her whole being yearned for it. She smiled at the congratulations of the Onslows. She gossiped with Spencer Cowper. She chatted with the Duke of Cambridge. And she danced in the arms of the Prince of Wales. That night she liked him and she laughed. She teased him, saying that she hoped that His Royal Highness did not find her as "evil-minded and malignant" as it was reported that he did. He must have found her otherwise, judging by the invitations which flowed to her in the following months.

After the ball was over, there was the pony trap in among all the smart equipages, and grand ladies were asking one another, Who was the tall young woman who drove herself in a trap and who was obviously on such good terms with the Prince of Wales?

The Princess had her last baby on 6th April 1871. Again it was a premature birth and nothing was ready at Sandringham—no nurse, no clothes. The boy lived for only twenty-four hours, just long enough for Mr Onslow to christen him Alexander John Charles Albert. The Prince was deeply upset and, with tears rolling down his cheeks, himself placed the tiny body in the coffin and arranged the white pall and the flowers.[9]

The effect on the mother was deeper still and more lasting. She had suffered pre-natal depression. The reason for this was said to have been that she was too active during her pregnancy, but in the event worry over her husband's behaviour and the events in which he had been involved was a main cause. Queen Victoria exacerbated matters by wishing the child to be buried at Windsor and Court mourning to be proclaimed. The Princess would have none of this, wishing her personal grief to remain private. So there was a simple funeral at Sandringham church and the baby was buried to the right of the path leading to the porch. Louise placed a bouquet of spring flowers on the grave.[10]

Alexandra and Louise now had a link to bind them, as they had both known the sadness of losing a baby. Thus it was that the Princess often made her way to Appleton, driving herself in the little carriage known as "the Blues". The well was filled with oranges for children whom she met on the road, and, as they came from school, they would clamber on to the carriage to save themselves the walk home.[11]

There were other worries. The Republican movement was gaining strength and there were some fifty Republican clubs in British cities and towns, including Cambridge and Norwich.[12] There were fears that Sandringham might become a target for the agitators and police protection was made available to farmers on the estate. Louise turned down the offer, but slept with a revolver under her pillow.

Certain newspapers were after the blood of the Prince of Wales. He was called a "louse" and it was forecast that he would never have the chance "to dishonour this country by becoming its King". The death of the baby Prince was described as "a wretched abortion", while the parents' grief and the child's funeral were labelled "sickening mummery at Sandringham".[13]

While the seeds of the Republican movement had come on the wind from France, both Queen Victoria and her eldest son provided fertile ground on which they could flourish in Britain. The Queen's seclusion was a primary cause of the discontent. Shut up at Windsor, Osborne or Balmoral, she provided no royal panorama, no "gilt and gingerbread". She received £385,000 a year but there was nothing to show for it. Although it was believed that she was piling up an immense fortune, she was "incessantly rattling the royal money box" and asking Parliament to provide marriage dowries for her "litter" of nine.[14] A pamphlet entitled *What does she do with it?* professed to make a thorough examination of her private income, and became a best-seller. Another cause of discontent and anger was the rôle of John Brown, the ghillie who guarded her door day and night.

The Prince of Wales, with his ladies and his gambling, was a sitting target. He was in Homburg in September and *Reynolds Newspaper* commented that "he was staking his gold upon the chances of a card or the roll of a ball—gold, be it remembered, that he obtained from the toil and sweat of the British workingman, without himself producing the value of a halfpenny. . . ."[15]

At the end of October the Prince and Princess stayed with Lady Londesborough at Londesborough Lodge near Scarborough. The drains were in a foul state and the Prince became infested with fever—"low fever, slow fever, gastric or bowel fever—they were all contemporary names for the dreaded typhoid fever".[16] Others infected were the Earl of Chesterfield and Charles Blegge, a groom from Sandringham. As the Wales returned to Norfolk to make ready for the Prince's birthday celebrations, Sir Charles Dilke made his famous speech at Newcastle. He attacked the Queen's dereliction of duty and urged his audience to be done with her and to set up a Republic. "Let it come," he roared.

On 23rd November it was announced that the Prince of Wales had typhoid fever. The headlines ran through the newspapers of the world, but Sandringham itself was hushed. Apart from anxiety about the Prince himself, there were other worries to consider. There were fears for the safety of local staff who had been at Londesborough, fears which became exaggerated when Blegge, the groom, died. There was speculation as to the future. If the Prince died, what would the future hold for those who were employed about the estate? Certain it was that the Princess would not be able to finance the running of Sandringham as a widow. If it was to be sold, could any landlord be found to continue running the place on the line which the Prince had laid down?

There was a special poignancy for Louise, for every anxious day brought back to her pictures of her husband's last illness. He had been near the same age as the Prince was now. Every evening she sent "the boy" up to the House to collect the latest bulletin and during the day, as she rode round her fields, she would glance towards the church to make sure that the flag was still flying.

> We heard of the excitement from without like the surging of the sea in the distance, but those who lived near or came from afar to hear the latest news were awed and hushed. . . .[17]

Never before had Wolferton station been so busy. On 29th November Queen Victoria stepped out of a special train and was driven up to Sandringham, the first time that she had visited her son's house. Satisfied with his condition, she returned next day to Windsor, but a week later was back in reply to an urgent summons.

"The Big House" bulged with royalties—two Princesses to one bed. Some of them proved to be a confounded nuisance. The Duke of Edinburgh and Prince Arthur refused to accept that their brother was really ill and wanted to get on with the shooting. The Duke of Cambridge pulled up manhole covers and sniffed around lavatories in the search for feverish smells. He cornered a man from the gas works and, without giving him a chance to reveal his identity, read him a lecture on the principles of plumbing. The Queen took over Sandringham in regimental sergeant-major fashion. Every day she trudged round in the slush and the snow and enquired about everything. She ordered the clocks to be put back to Greenwich time, dismissing the Prince's practice as "nonsense".[18]

The most discordant voice around the sick bed was that of Princess Alice. She was two years younger than the Prince of Wales and his favourite sister. It was she who had nursed the Prince Consort through his last illness. Since that time she had had further experience while nursing the wounded in hospitals during two wars—the Seven weeks war and the Franco-Prussian. She had witnessed sights the details of which she dare not confide to her mother. She was a disciple of Florence Nightingale. She was a friend of David Friederich Strauss, biblical critic and man of letters. As a result of her hospital work and her talks with Strauss, Alice lost her faith in God.[19] She was by far the most experienced nurse at Sandringham, but her godlessness and the discipline of a matron found favour neither with the Princess of Wales nor the Queen. Alice quashed "Alix". When the "divine providence" was mentioned, Alice burst out: "Providence, there is no Providence, no nothing, but I can't think how anyone can talk such rubbish."[20] Although Queen Victoria often took exception to the acts of the Almighty, she was not prepared to go to the lengths of declaring war. Alice's popularity slipped fast.

But there were times when it was tactful to keep the inexperienced Princess of Wales out of the sickroom. Some of her husband's bouts of raving were not for her ears—"all sort of revelations and names of people mentioned".[21] At times he longed for her, at others the sight of her enraged him. Once she crept into his room on all fours, but, when she rose, he floored her with a pillow.

Yet the Princess knew enough about his other life by now. During one of his quiet periods, she addressed him as "my good boy". He reminded her that he was her husband and she replied: "That was once but is no more. You have broken your vows."[22]

On 13th December the Queen and Princess Alice were certain that the end had come, that the tenth anniversary of the death of the Prince Consort would be the last day in the life of his eldest son. The message had come to Louise the day before. "If the Prince could but sleep, all might be well". But he did not sleep. Out of her own experience she guessed that he was slipping. But the miracle happened and altered history. Next morning she saw the flag still flying on the tower of Sandringham church. During the day Albert Edward drank three glasses of ale and the crisis was over. So was Republicanism.

A service of national thanksgiving for the Prince's recovery was held at St Paul's Cathedral on 27th February, the Queen and her family driving in a semi-state procession from Buckingham

Palace. This was the last occasion on which the Sovereign was received by the Lord Mayor at Temple Bar with the traditional ceremonies, the gates being first shut against her and then opened.[23]*

But before the Prince and Princess left for London, Sandringham had a little occasion of its own. Louise and a fellow tenant, Mr James Freeman, had composed "a very respectful and affectionate address", and the written copy, illuminated on vellum and signed by every householder on the estate, was placed in a casket of carved oak. The presentation was made on 6th February and the Rector read out the message.[24] It was too much for the Princess.

> She broke down in the speech she made in return, and Mr Onslow nearly did the same, and I think we all felt—I do not know exactly how.[25]

SOURCES

1 Cathcart: *Sandringham*, p. 91
2 Longford: *Victoria R.I.*, p. 376
3 Dennis: *Coronation Commentary*, p. 17
4 Longford: *Victoria R.I.*, p. 379
5 Bullock: *Crowned to Serve*
6 Maurois: *King Edward and His Times*, p. 75
7 Sanderson: *King Edward VII*, Vol. II, p. 161
8 Ibid.
9 Battiscombe: *Queen Alexandra*, p. 112
10 *The Graphic*
11 Paul: *Britain's King and Queen*, p. 287
12 Magnus: *King Edward the Seventh*, p. 146
13 Dennis: *Coronation Commentary*, p. 17
14 Ibid.
15 24th September 1871
16 Longford: *Victoria R.I.*, p. 297
17 Cresswell, p. 187
18 Ponsonby: *Henry Ponsonby*, p. 99
19 Duff: *Hessian Tapestry*, pp. 166–7
20 Battiscombe: *Queen Alexandra*, p. 117
21 Ibid., p. 115
22 Ibid.
23 Lee: *Queen Victoria*, p. 414
24 *The Graphic*; Sanderson: *King Edward VII*, Vol. II, p. 175
25 Cresswell, p. 189

* Six years later the Bar was removed and sold to Sir Henry Meux, who re-erected it at his home of Theobalds Park, Hertfordshire. Its site in Fleet Street was marked by a memorial, bearing on it statues of Queen Victoria and the then Prince of Wales.

14
Church Affairs

Morning Service at Sandringham was a Church parade, at least while the Prince was in residence. One Sunday afternoon, when he was inspecting the stables as was his wont, he reprimanded a groom for being absent from Matins. "I always attend myself," he said, "and I expect my people to do the same."[1]

Yet Albert Edward cheated. While the Princess and the ladies drove to church at eleven o'clock, he only attended the second part of the service which began at a quarter to twelve. He, and menfolk of like thinking, would stroll across the park. On reaching the churchyard, all followed the royal example, placing their walking sticks against a particular tombstone.[2] The royal progress had been kept under observation and the bell rang as a signal of his arrival. The Prince would then tiptoe in to join the congregation, "looking", as his grandson, the Duke of Windsor, said, "as if he had been detained by matters of great importance".[3] Louise commented that he appeared bored and was obviously glad when the proceedings were over, "which is better than . . . appearing to be devout when you are not".[4]

Sunday was the only "day off" in the week for her. It was a day of real rest, disturbed only by the arrival of calves, foals and lambs. There was nothing gloomy about the Sandringham Sabbath, nothing to be seen of the contemporary custom of drawing the blinds and reading only religious books. The Prince saw to that, and Louise was in agreement with him. In the event it brought her the main excitement of the week, for at St Mary Magdalene's she could observe at close quarters prime ministers and current heroes, bishops and foreign potentates, dukes and their duchesses, jockeys and boxers, dandies and wits, actresses and the cream of the Jews. She came face to face with men and women who would otherwise have been but names in the columns of *The Times*.

The notabilities apart, Louise liked the service. It was simple and it was hearty. The Reverend William Lake Onslow, chaplain

R.N., had spent most of his life at sea and, before coming to Sandringham, had been naval instructor to Prince Alfred. There was more of the "Salt" about him that the "Parson" and he came from a naval family. His grandfather, Vice-Admiral Sir Richard Onslow, had been knighted for gallantry during Lord Duncan's victory off Camperdown in 1797. His father had commanded the corvette *Daphne*, while his three brothers had all joined the Service, dying at sea at the ages of nineteen, twenty-five and twenty-six.

Louise was a stern critic of religion. In comparing the Sandringham services with others, she wrote:

> Many a dreary Sunday morning have I sat with frozen feet and hands through the drawled-out and gabbled prayers, the ill-sung hymns, and the tedious, lifeless sermon. . . .[5]

She studied the different creeds, finding the Methodists somewhat too fond of money and the Wesleyans more suited to the towns than the countryside. She was intrigued by the Ranters, the nickname for the Primitive Methodists. Here was the spirit of revivalism, racy and lively. She noticed a reaction among the village children. While they would try every trick, and make any excuse, to get out of going to Church, they would cry if they were forbidden to attend a Meeting of the Ranters. Louise wanted to know how the preachers managed to send the girls into fits and hysterics, and to organise the hand clapping and shouting, but to attend a local Meeting was more than even she dared to do. She had been in enough trouble at Appleton as it was and did not fancy the label of "Ranter" tied round her neck. So she moved outside the area and joined in a Whitsuntide feast and "kiss-in". She treasured some of the Ranters' sayings:

On Contentment
"Here, my friends, be the quality—a given fourteen pence a pound for lamb, and yew come here and get the lamb of God for nothen."

On Strife
"They was all a quarrellen'; one says, I'm for Paul, another says I ain't, 'I'm for Cephas, and another for summon else. Paul he hears on it, and down he comes and sune squares 'em all up. You don't belong to me, says he, you don't belong to none on us, only to the Lord."

On Disobedience
"After the Lord had made Adam and Eve out of the clay, he put 'em in a garden for to dress it and keep it, and he calls 'em

up and says, 'Look you here, Adam and Eve,' says he, 'you've got this here garden for yer very own, to do just what yer like with it; you may have pears, and plums, and strawberries and all sorts o'things, and make jam or what yer please, but yer ain't to touch this here tree, *them's* my winter apples.'" This was followed by a vigorous piece of play-acting representing the sin and discovery of the culprits and their ultimate expulsion into the thorns and briars of the wilderness.

One speaker announced that he was so happy in the light of the Lord that, if they were to put him in a barrel and nail down the top, he would shout "Hallelujah" through the bung-hole. Doubtless, if Albert Edward had sneaked off with Louise, he would have enjoyed the "kiss-in" just as much as she did.

St Mary Magdalene's had its lighter moments, but of a differing kind. Church affairs were handled by the Rector and the Princess. They were close friends but somewhat in awe of the Prince, who regarded himself as the figure-head of God and was apt to be dictatorial. Thus it was that at times they conspired together to maintain the peace.

The organist was a village tradesman. He was conscientious and proud of his job, but his capabilities were strictly limited. As the Prince Consort had been an organist of considerable merit, the Prince considered himself a pundit on the matter. One Sunday he decided that he could stomach the local talent no longer and accordingly ordered the Rector and his wife to dismiss the tradesman and replace him with someone more accomplished. The two of them went into discussion and came to the conclusion that "it would not be quite kind to send him away in such a hurry and hurt his feelings". Alexandra could not bear to hurt people's feelings—unless the people were Germans. They therefore devised a little scheme. The tradesman should stay on in his job and efforts would be made to improve his playing. Then his presence would not cause comment and he would be able to stay. Meantime, if accosted, they were to say that they were having difficulty in finding a replacement.

Two Sundays passed and the Prince made no comment. For the third Sunday Mr Gladstone was a guest at Sandringham. His Old Testament face, his beaky nose, his steely eyes, proved too great a strain for the tradesman at the organ. He was hynotised. The last lines of "Rock of Ages", Gladstone's favourite hymn, coincided with the most ghastly caterwauling from the pipes, and the howling and the groaning went on long after the whispered "Amen" should have slipped away into silence.

All eyes turned to the Prince. He was flushed and showing signs of difficulty in controlling his emotions. At the close of the service he strode quickly from the church and took up his stance on the grass beyond. The Rector moved to the door to pass greetings with his congregation. The Princess held back and threw him an appealing look. "Come here, both of you," roared the Prince. They shuffled up together, penitent, before all the flock. They "caught it good and proper".

Back at the Rectory, Louise giggled over her Madeira. For a change, the boot was on the other foot. She told Mr Onslow that he should be proud to be crucified in the company of such a companion, that many people would consider it a high honour to share with the lovely Princess of Wales the bracket of "both of you". But poor Mr Onslow could not see the funny side of being "bawled out" in front of the G.O.M.

Many of the great speakers of the day preached at Sandringham. Louise considered that Arthur Stanley, Dean of Westminster, who had accompanied the Prince on his tour of the Holy Land in 1862, was the most impressive. His Lordship of Oxford, Dr Wilberforce, was too theatrical. Charles Kingsley was on his best behaviour and it was difficult to reconcile him with "Parson Lot", the Chartists' Champion. Louise came to the conclusion that the Princess and her children had made such a fuss of him that "you feel that no one but a brute could wish to upset the monarchy". Dr Magee, Bishop of Peterborough, provided a feast of grand oratory and carried his audience away with him. For his own part, Dr Magee, who was a guest in December 1873, found a visit to Sandringham an enlightening experience. He wrote:

> I arrived just as they were all at tea in the entrance hall, and had to walk in all seedy and dishevelled from my day's journey and sit down by the Princess of Wales. I find the company pleasant and civil, but we are a curious mixture. Two Jews, Sir Anthony de Rothschild and his daughter;* an ex-Jew, Disraeli; a Roman Catholic, Colonel Higgins; an Italian duchess who is an Englishwoman, and her daughter, brought up a Roman Catholic and now turning Protestant; a set of young lords and a bishop. . . .[6]

Louise's favourite in the pulpit was that great sporting parson, "Jack" Russell. "He brought a Devonshire breeze with him, and you thought of Dartmoor, and Exmoor, and Whyte Melville and Katerfelto. . . ."[7] She understood him best and felt at home with

---

* Afterwards Lady Battersea.

him. He was also a favourite of the Princess of Wales, who made him comfortable with "port wine and the twice of fish".

One fashionable preacher from a London parish was not a success at Sandringham. He was very voluble and, as one of the congregation said afterwards, "tew much o'the ranter". His sermon dealt with the importance of righteousness and temperance, and stress was put on the punishment which awaited those who erred and strayed. There was no direct criticism of the way of life of the Prince, but he got the message. He was in some doubt as to the reaction of the cleric if he learned that it was royal custom to repair to the bowling alley as soon as the clock struck midnight on the seventh day. The Prince therefore gave out a general impression that he was going to bed early that night and his guest, taking the hint, retired to his room. Once he was out of the way, the fun began in the alley. Unfortunately, next morning at breakfast, one of the guests, who was not addicted to bowls, remarked to the cleric: "I say, you *were* a lucky fellow last night. They pinned me down there in the bowling alley till four o'clock this morning."

One of the most memorable mornings at Sandringham church was the occasion of the christening, and admission to the Christian faith, of Princess Alexandra's *enfant terrible*, her Abyssinian coffee-boy. She had "collected" him during her visit to Egypt in 1868. She had also "collected" a very ugly sheep. It had gnawed through its mooring rope in the stern of the Nile steamer and wandered off on the scrounge. It came across H.R.H. lying in a long chair and dreaming dreams in the desert night. It put its cold nose on her knee and shook her considerably. When an irate and blood-thirsty cook arrived on the scene, the Princess learned that the animal was reserved for the next day's dinner. By this time she had struck up a friendship with the sheep and resolutely refused to eat it. It was shipped back to the Norfolk pastures and thereafter known as "the Princess's sheep". The sheep proved less nuisance than the boy.

Alexandra saw the boy's face in the light of a camp fire and was intrigued by the ivory teeth and the broad smile. She coveted him. Her sister-in-law, the "bossy" Alice, had a Malay boy, why should she not have an Abyssinian? There were no obstacles. His father was unknown, believed dead. It was rumoured that his mother was a whore in Cairo, whose hands were too occupied to cope with an "unfortunate mistake". There was even doubt about his name, this being given as Ali Achmet,[8] Hakim,[9] and Selim,[10] but Selim was used in his occasional mentions in the Court Circular, so Selim he shall be. Turned out to fend for himself, the ten-year-old had become a donkey-boy, relying on the pickings from the rich tourists exploring the Nile. He had acquired certain essential words of the English language. He was sent back, with the sheep, to Sandringham. There, arrayed in native dress, his duties were to serve coffee and clean pipes.

The country folk of Norfolk were unaccustomed to meeting Abyssinians and were considerably alarmed. Appreciating his shock potential, Selim would jump out from behind bushes upon the unsuspecting. Louise's pony was even more alarmed than she was. With time on his hands, Selim moved from mischief to mischief. He chanced upon a large and coloured umbrella, the property of Alfred, Duke of Edinburgh. Aware that such adornment was the pride of the chiefs of Africa, he strode up and down before Sandringham House, the umbrella raised above him. While at Marlborough House he sallied forth into St James's: he entered a fashionable establishment selling ties, ordered forty of the best and put them down to the royal account. This hit the Prince in a soft spot and he decided that the only cure for the boy was to bring him into the safety of the Christian faith. Accordingly Selim was sent to Mr Onslow for preparatory instruction prior to the baptismal ceremonial. The Rector was delighted with the quickness with which "his little heathen" mastered the catechism and scripture lessons. Yet Selim was not above twisting the new found knowledge to his own advantage. When questioned by the housekeeper as to the wording of the Eighth Commandment, he replied: "Thou shalt have no other gods but *me*."

On a Sunday morning early in December 1872, Louise was among the crowded congregation in Sandringham church. The Bishop of Winchester was to preach and among the house-guests was the Duke of Edinburgh. A note was passed round the pews, giving permission for those who so desired to stay on for the baptism of Selim. Louise stayed. The Prince, Princess and Sir W. Knollys were the sponsors. The Prince presented the boy to the Bishop, naming him "Albert Alexander" after his royal godfather and godmother.[11] With a feeling of a job well done, the royal party returned to lunch.

Yet there had been no true conversion. Selim moved towards his finest hour. Arrayed in "the Jagers Highland costume", he took one of his master's Purdy's and disappeared into the woods. The keepers heard shooting but were unable to trace the culprit. Next day the Prince headed a battue. He raised his gun and pulled the trigger, but nothing happened. Selim had broken the firing mechanism. The gunsmiths were in jeopardy, but fortunately someone had spotted Selim sneaking away into the woods. The Prince summoned the Rector and the household and, before them, threatened Selim with the penitentiary if he did not mend his ways. For a while the law proved more potent than the Church, but soon Selim was up to his tricks again. The Prince became convinced that his wife had brought back an evil spirit from the banks of the Nile. Selim disappeared and Louise saw him no more. It was rumoured that he had been sent to a clergyman to be exorcised. Louise was sorry for him, for, with a long experience of "backus boys" behind her, she recognised pure mischief when she saw it.

SOURCES

1   Cathcart: *Sandringham*, p. 139
2   Wortham: *The Delightful Profession*, p. 197
3   Cathcart: *Sandringham*, p. 139
4   Cresswell, p. 144
5   Cresswell: *Norfolk and the Squires* etc., p. 23
6   Macdonnell: *Life of William Connor Magee*, Vol. I, pp. 293–4
7   Cresswell, p. 147
8   Magnus: *King Edward the Seventh*, p. 137
9   Cresswell
10   *The Graphic*, 14th December 1872
11   Ibid.

15
High Society

The Prince of Wales brought a social revolution to Norfolk. He cut through the class structure which had existed for centuries and he upset many of the County families. The primary reason for his so doing was that he was unfamiliar with that structure. He had had no chance to learn of it and to become imbued. As a boy he had been kept behind the thorn hedge which surrounded royalty and thus never learned the table of values and priorities inescapable in an English public school. On educational tours he had been kept under the strict eye of a Governor and he knew more of the Continent than of Britain. At Oxford and Cambridge he had been little more than a prisoner, and his only "fling" had been in Canada and America. Sandringham provided his first true taste of the way of life of the English people.

His father's attitude had influenced him. Albert was a German, and said openly: "I shall never cease to be a true German."[1] To emphasise the point he made it again in his native tongue—"*ein treuer Deutscher, Coburger, Gothaner zu sein*".[2] He was for ever pointing out to his sons that profligacy and laziness were inherent in the young men of Society. He made no effort to mix with, or understand, the members of the aristocracy, and accordingly they declared war on him. As Lord Lennox remarked to Sir Henry Cole after the Prince Consort's death, "Truth to say, the 'Swells', as a class, did not much like the P. . . ."[3] Although he was at loggerheads with his father, Albert Edward could not be expected to understand, or take seriously, an unwritten table of precedence for county families. His yardstick was the *Almanach de Gotha*, coupled with the amount of money in the bank.

There were three big annual balls at Sandringham, the County, the Farmers' and the Servants', and it was over the first of these that the Prince ran into trouble. The County people, or the "elect" as Louise called them, considered that invitations should be restricted to themselves and to those whom they chose to

introduce. The Prince thought otherwise and crammed Sandringham with a motley crowd.

There has always been, and ever will be, conflict between those
who hold advantage from the established order and those who
do not, the former wishing to retain and the latter to destroy.
The latter win in the end as they are vastly superior in numbers.
And, having won, they then seek for themselves the advantage
of a newly established order of their own making. An exaggerated
example of this struggle was to be seen in Norfolk in the
1860–70s. The county had been invaded by industrial magnates
from the North, who had made their money in railways and
engineering, coal and cotton. They were not as yet accepted by
the squirearchy, but they were determined that they soon would
be, and they had the money to back them. The "smart, rich"
farmers, who had benefited from war prices, joined them, seeking promotion from the Farmers' to the County ball, one rung
up the stackyard ladder. It was these people who made Albert
Edward's policy possible—if he had tried it thirty years before,
in the days of Wellington and Melbourne, he would have "got a
bloody nose".

The Squiresses went on strike and boycotted the County ball.
There was talk of "how common Royalty was becoming" and
that "one had to draw a line somewhere". The Prince noted the
absent faces and was furious. Without the "elect" the County ball
had no right to be so called. He cornered certain of the truants
and read them the Riot Act. He mixed the charm of his wheedling
with the cold shadow of the threat. The result was that the Prince
was allowed to ask whom he chose, within reason, and in return
the "elect" were invited, in their exclusiveness, to the strictly
private occasions, and were asked to join the house-party for
the junior balls, being received in the drawing-room, walking in
the procession to the ballroom and taking part in the opening
quadrille.

But even this solution to the tricky problem did not bring uni-
versal peace. We move to the level of Brown, Jones, and Robinson, ever watchful for the chance to gain foothold in "the Big
House". One morning, to his delight, Brown receives an invitation
to attend the County ball. His womenfolk swoon with delight
and hurry off to Norwich or London to order their gowns. Nose
in air, Brown makes an excuse to call on Robinson, intent on
making casual, and telling, reference to the honour which has
come his way. On Robinson's chimney-piece he sees a similar

invitation from Sandringham. Deflated, Mrs and the Misses Brown declare that "one must draw a line somewhere".

Those less fortunate than Brown and Robinson redoubled their efforts to obtain invitations, and none were more determined than the local clergy. It was known that Mr Onslow had certain influence and the poor man's life became a nightmare. Louise dismissed the efforts and the schemings of the tuft-hunters as trivial and stupid, but she had to watch her step, for there was no easier way to make a mortal enemy than to upset the social climb. There were many people who suspected that there was more between the Prince and Mrs Cresswell than met the eye, an impression, which, at this time, the Prince was doing nothing to contradict. She had to resist sternly those who importuned her to obtain invitations, but she was, in fact, in view of her local knowledge, being used to "vet" applications from people unknown to the Sandringham staff. She kept that a close secret, but commented: "I won't put my foot in a wasps' nest by relating the manœuvres and devices resorted to by people who you would have thought were above such things."[4]

Louise did everything in her power to avoid having her name coupled with that of the Prince of Wales. It became almost a fetish with her. It might have suited her book better had she not been quite so circumspect. The Prince certainly opened the door for her, but she would not come through.

> It was a pity that opportunity fell upon the wrong person instead of someone with money and leisure to avail herself of it, and who could have followed it up through London seasons and Marlborough House.[5]

Louise was allowed to ask whom she liked to the County ball and it was one of the few occasions during the year when all the bedrooms at Appleton were full. One year she took a newly married couple. The Prince took a fancy to them, or at least to the bride. He asked Louise to bring them to a more select entertainment held a few days later.

> It was one of those evenings when the "elect" were kept penned up in such a hot ante-room that, excepting for the honour of the thing, I would rather have been outside, until the drawing-room door was thrown open and we marched in single file and made our reverence to the Royalties, like the London Drawing-room in miniature.[6]

Louise made her deep curtsey and was rising from "the depths of the earth" when the Prince asked her to wait and introduce her friends when they came up. Now the newly weds were young and very junior and way back in the queue. The long line came on and eyes opened wide in astonishment as it was noted that, beside the Heir to the Throne, in his gayest mood, stood the pretty widow from Appleton, looking, for all the world, as if she would end up as the Queen of England.

There was another night when she felt the daggers cutting into her back. The guests, many distinguished, had been ushered into an ante-room and were waiting to be called, looking around to determine their own precedence. The Comptroller, not being extensively acquainted with the local society, had a temporary lapse of memory and forgot the names of them all. Then he recognised Louise and went into action. "Mrs Gerard Cresswell," he announced. Louise was hypnotised. From all corners of the room hostile eyes were fixed upon her. She wanted to argue and explain, but the Royalties were waiting and she just had to march. There was little wonder that the tongues tattled.

Louise was a shy person. Living alone and being fully occupied with her farm, she had no social round of her own. Thus she looked forward to the Sandringham occasions as her only form of relaxation. But she liked to be submerged in the crowd, observing unobserved, and dreaded the limelight being turned upon her. Then she shrivelled. She found the private parties somewhat formidable.

One day when the Prince was shooting near Appleton he called in at the house and asked Louise if she would like to come to a little dance that he was arranging that night. It was in the nature of a "command" and she said yes. He invited any guests that she had, but there were none—there seldom were—so she had to face the lone entrance. But she had progressed as far as having a "coachman", so at least she had the comfort of the brougham.

Alone in the corridor of "the Big House", her courage slipped away at the thought of being ushered into the drawing-room. Fortunately one of the Equerries passed by and, guessing her fears, took her by the arm and led her in.

The Princess's Danish relations were there, the Duke of Cambridge, the Duke and Duchess of Teck and, among the non-royals, Lord Henry Lennox and Gerald Wellesley, Dean of Windsor. The Prince introduced Louise to the Dean, who was "particularly pleasant". Now deans have long had the gift of integrating themselves with the royal family, becoming cosy confidants and father confessors, as distinct from lofty bishops who are apt to pass judgment, possibly provide rebuke and perhaps seek change of appointment. No one knew the weaknesses of the Prince of Wales better than the Dean of Windsor.

Supper was served at a long, narrow table, the royal gaggle being at the centre. The Dean took Louise in. The Dean was placed next to the royals and on the same side as the host and hostess. He immediately became one of them. Louise felt a little shaky and concentrated on the food and monosyllables.

A gaggle of royals at full gas is, at best, a terrifying confrontation. It was much more so in the nineteenth century than the twentieth. Earl Mountbatten has described them as a trade union. To any one outside the union, the conversation was hard to follow.

Names seemed to form a code—Lenchen and Looloo, Baby and Pussy, Franz and Frittie and Fritz, Willie and Wally, Ella, Ditta and Uncle E. Places were determined by palaces—Babelsberg and Bernstorff, Rumpenheim and Rheinhardsbrunn, Tatoi and Laeken, Kranichstein, Juggenheim and Illinskoje. Louise knew the names of all her cows, but this continental miscellany was beyond her.

Suddenly the babble ceased and there was silence. Maybe an angel passed, or it was twenty past, or they all ran out of breath. And in the silence the eyes of the man sitting opposite to Louise fell upon her.

He was a very handsome man, tall and well built. His hair was so black that, in the lamplight, it shone as dark blue. Below his high forehead were beautiful and kindly eyes. Beneath his waxed moustachios was "a little tuft of an imperial". In Vienna he was known as *der schöne Uhlan*.[7] His name was Francis of Teck and he had but recently been upped to Duke. He was the husband of George of Cambridge's stout sister, Mary Adelaide, known as "Fat Mary" and taking her place in history as the mother of Queen Mary.

The Duke addressed Louise. He apologised, elegantly, profusely, for not having recognised her earlier. He was a Prince from Strauss and he might well have been at *Schönbrunn* begging the forgiveness of the Empress Elizabeth. All royal eyes and ears concentrated on the polished performance.

Louise prayed that her chair might descend through the floor into the game larder or whatever lay below. She was "covered with confusion as with a cloke". As the blood rushed to her cheeks, she blundered out some answer and then promptly forgot what she had said. In the nights to come she lay awake trying to determine how big an ass she had made of herself.

She was not always shy—it depended on those who were about

her. Her greatest conquest was Bernal Osborne. Ralph Bernal
Osborne was a wit and rather wicked. An advanced Liberal
politician, he could convulse a party with his instantaneous jokes
and droll facial expressions.[8] He was therefore in much demand
with hostesses and was the favourite social jester of Albert Edward. He was no respecter of royal persons, even when inside
Sandringham, and therefore in sympathy with Louise. To have a
tête-à-tête with him was a coveted honour. One night he chatted
to Louise for a solid half hour. She felt the daggers again. She
thought that he had done it just to make the others jealous.

She was at ease with the Duke of Cambridge. He always made
a point of chatting with her when he came down on his week's
holiday. On one occasion the Prince listened in. The Duke simply
could not understand how any woman could choose to live alone
and farm. He put Louise through a catechism about it. He insisted
that she recite everything that she did throughout the day. The
cross-examination being completed, he asked:

"But the evening, Mrs Cresswell, the evening. Now what do
you do in the evening?"

"I have the accounts, Sir, and the work to think about."

"But what an isolated life. Have you no neighbours now, neighbours?"

"Yes, Sir, very nice neighbours."

"And then you say times are so bad. Now what will you do
about that?"

"I think, Sir, His Royal Highness won't get any rent!" She
flashed a glance at the Prince and saw that he was "grinning
amazingly".

Dancing at Sandringham had its dangers. The floors were highly
polished and the Prince was an enthusiastic performer, his guests
following his example. As he urged Louise to let herself go, he
remarked, "I like to dance to the tune." But she danced but seldom and had no intention of ending flat on her back for the
benefit and delectation of the Heir to the Throne. She had a
narrow escape when "going down the middle" at full gallop with
Henry Villebois, the robust ex-master of the West Norfolk. His
feet went out underneath him and he crashed to the floor. She
was half down before she managed to escape his grip. Sir Anthony
de Rothschild was another menace. The jovial old Jew had a fine
sense of timing but a poor sense of direction and, when steamed
up, would caper off in any direction which caught his fancy.
Louise would then have to run over and fetch him back, an act
which thoroughly upset the Royal Quadrille, which was taken

rather seriously. But she could forgive Sir Anthony anything, as he was a good customer for her pigs.

Of all the annual entertainments Louise liked the Servants' ball best of all. So did the Prince, for then he was undisputed master and, like his grandson, the Duke of Windsor, he was more at home in the sergeants' mess than in the officers'. A number of retired royal retainers had been given cottages at Sandringham and their memories went back to the days of George IV and William IV. They brought back the dignity and splendour of "the good old days" and it was a treat to watch them tread the minuet. On occasion the staff of Marlborough House would come down, showing off the latest fashions and retailing London gossip. Then there were contrasting sights which brought a smile—such as the mass of the Duchess of Teck cavorting with the Princess's coach-man, the smallest man on the floor.

The ball opened with a country dance, the Prince and Princess leading off with the heads of the respective departments. . . . The house-party, equerries, ladies-in-waiting, and all invited from the neighbourhood, were ordered to join in, no shirking or sitting out allowed, and when the sides had been made up, the Prince and the Princess set off with their partners, round and round, down the middle and up again, and so on to the end, the Prince the jolliest of the jolly. . . . His own Master of the Ceremonies, signalling and sending messages to the band, arranging every dance, and when to begin and when to leave off, noticing the smallest mistake in the figures, and putting people in their places. In the "Triumph", which is such an exhausting dance, he looked as if he could have gone on all night and into the middle of next week. . . . He is an anti-dote to every text and sermon that ever was preached upon the pleasures of the world palling upon the wearied spirit. . . . It was a mercy to have a Quadrille now and then for a little rest. The Marl-borough housekeeper, who was attired in a pea-green silk, danced it in the old polite style, holding up her gown in points, and drop-ping a little curtsey to her partner each time she came forward, like Mrs Fazziwig* of immortal memory. Then a jig was started, and it was so pretty to see the way the Princess danced it, while the state liveries of the footmen and green velvet of the game-keepers and Highland costumes, mixed up with the scarlet coats of the country gentlemen, and the lovely toilettes and the merry tune, made a sight to be seen or heard. Almost before one dance ended, the Prince started another, and suddenly the Scotch pipers would screech out and the Prince would fold his arms and fling himself into a Highland fling, and so on fast and furious until far into the small hours of the morning, with supper intervening, when

* Of "*A Christmas Carol*", by Charles Dickens.

our former partners, the footmen, waited upon everyone as demurely as if they had not at all been careering about together just before.[9]

Louise admitted that she might have antiquated ideas, but she did not approve of the young girls waltzing with the grooms. "Country dances are all very well, but not the round and rounds."[10] She feared that contact with the hot and vibrant parts of the female chassis might awaken ideas better restricted to the inmates of the stables.

She watched with interest the differing treatment accorded to royal guests. If the Prince wished to impress, there could be no more thoughtful host. He would go as far as stoking the bedroom fire and checking the temperature of the water in the jugs. A gouty old squire, who had no respect for a new-comer, royal or no, was completely won over by finding that he had been allotted a ground floor room to save him the pain and strain of a climb up the stairs.[11] A Sandringham weekend acted as a "patent conjuring machine" on the Left wing, a Republican being stuffed in at one end and a Courtier squeezed out at the other. Henry Broadhurst, M.P., the Prince's Radical colleague on the Royal Commission on the Housing of the Working Classes, was truly converted. Not being equipped to "change" for dinner, he was served in his own rooms. He later commented that he "left Sandringham with a feeling of one who had spent a weekend with an old chum of his own rank in society. . . ."[12]

Perhaps Louise had Christopher Sykes in mind when she wrote:

> On the other hand, with the extraordinary variety of character that H.R.H. presents, those who are invited as butts and buffoons and the recipients of practical jokes have rather a rough time of it, though if they prefer to go in that way rather than not go at all, they have no one but themselves to blame.[13]

One who fell between the two stools was Mr Gladstone. He could look after himself, and was too good a whist player for the Prince's liking, but he had to put up with the chaff. A drawing of him appeared on a screen in the billiard room. He was in company with other eminent Victorians, such as Matthew Arnold and Lord Salisbury. All were displayed in "very dubious attitudes". They were being attended to by a company of nude ladies.[14] A non-smoker, the G.O.M. was persuaded to experiment. He immediately blew smoke down his nose in imitation of his host.[15] His poor wife fared little better, being inveigled into the bowling alley and there forced to take unaccustomed exercise.[16]

A great feature of the winter entertainment was the skating. There were parties every night and Louise was invited to come as she wished. This was fairyland. Torches flared round the edge of Sandringham's lake and coloured lights hung from the trees. A band played on the island and fireworks added magic and excitement to the scene.[17] The villagers were given leave to watch and clustered together at the end of the lake away from the house, the murmur of their talk and laughter broadcast into the frosty night. Swift-moving figures showed for a moment in the torch-lit paths across the ice, and then were swallowed in the darkness; and the tiny lights on the skating chairs shone like glowworms.

Louise did not join the skaters. Her skill was limited and she feared contrast with the expert Princess who, a dream of beauty in her Siberian style costume and cap, floated around the lake arm-in-arm with one of her ladies. She had no wish to sample the indignity of being trundled round in a chair. She was happy just to watch, hands in muff.

She was standing alone one evening when the Prince sought her out. The moving picture had lulled her into a trance and she knew not how long she had been there. He asked if she was not frozen stiff from standing there so long, and added, "Do you *never* skate?" Then off he hurried to the refreshment tent and returned with two tumblers of negus.* It brought a glow and was most welcome.

Soon afterwards Louise met a man friend and he teased her.

"Pretty rowdy lot you were on the ice the other night, your old nurse tippling with the shoemaker at one end of the lake, and you drinking negus with the Prince at the other."[18]

Louise saw a danger light flickering and she did not attend the skating again. The Prince was watching out for her and the next time he rode through Appleton farm, he stopped and said to her, in his pointed and accusing way: "You never came to the skating again."

She gave no answer, and just looked away.

SOURCES

1 Arthur: *Concerning Queen Victoria and Her Son*, p. 47
2 *Early Years of the Prince Consort*, p. 103
3 Ames: *Prince Albert and Victorian Taste*, p. 175

* Wine, hot water, sugar and spices.

4   Cresswell, p. 163
5   Ibid., p. 167
6   Ibid., p. 174
7   Pope-Hennessey: *Queen Mary*, p. 37
8   Battersea: *Reminiscences*, p. 107
9   Cresswell, pp. 169–71
10 Ibid., p. 171
11 Wortham: *The Deljghtful Profession*, p. 194
12 Magnus: *King Edward the Seventh*, p. 229
13 Cresswell, p. 168
14 Wrotham: *The Delightful Profession*, p. 193
15 Cathcart: *Sandringham*, p. 114
16 Drew: *Catherine Gladstone*, p. 103
17 Sanderson: *King Edward VII*, Vol. II, p. 161
18 Cresswell, p. 181

16

Beloved Lady

The portrait of Alexandra has been smeared by the dirty thumbs of time. Among the printed words of recent years can be found insinuations that she was stupid, selfish, stubborn, lacking in mental power and artistic appreciation and over-obsessed with her children. In life no woman was ever more adored and praised. As already observed, it was Bernal Osborne who said of her, as Princess of Wales, that it was she who kept the Throne for her husband.[1]

Those who saw stupidity were not making fair allowance for the disadvantages of deafness. If there were signs of stubborness there, it was because she had married into an arrogant and argumentative family, with strong German bias, who openly admitted that they disliked her Danish relations. Often stubbornness was her only means of defence. Selfish? What other course was open to a woman married to a man such as Albert Edward but to retreat into, and uprate the value of, self? If she had not, she would have lost both her identity and her pride. Certainly she had not the powers of research and argument possessed by her sisters-in-law, Victoria and Alice, but they were in the advance guard of "Women's Lib", meddling with affairs beyond their scope and heading for terminal tragedy. Alexandra had no wish to be liberated; she found fulfilment in children and dogs and horses, in love of humanity and clean laughter. That she spoiled her children was in part due to the restricted relationship with her husband and in part because it was the custom of her family so to do. It happened in Denmark, Russia and Greece.

A woman of the loveliness of Alexandra of natural course aroused jealousies in her own sex, just as she enrolled disciples among all manner of men. But if ill judgment is made of her, there must also be recalled the rift which split the Royal Family at the end of the nineteenth century. On one side was the "Sandringham Set", consisting of the Wales in full force, Princess

Louise, Marchioness of Lorne, and young Prince Leopold for a time. They backed Denmark and France and were tied to Russia. On the other was the "Osborne Set", or "German Set", composed of the mass of Queen Victoria's offspring, all linked to Germany, the Hesses, the Duke of Saxe-Coburg and Gotha, Princess Beatrice, and, in particular, the Christians. They were stirred up, and whipped on, by young William of Germany, ever seeking a chance to deflate his "Uncle Bertie". As the Marquess of Carisbrooke remarked: "The rivalry was incredible—you would never believe it."[2] But it was clear to see when the Kaiser and the Prince of Wales raced their yachts against one another. When the two "Sets" came face to face at the funeral of Prince Albert Victor, war was near to breaking out in St George's Chapel, Windsor.[3] If Alexandra's logic is called in doubt, it must be remembered that Britain would have been wise to listen to her warning as to the aims of Germany. When war was declared in 1914, she took her son, the King, by the lapels of his coat, shook him and shouted: "I told you so! I told you that Willie was the very devil!"

Louise Cresswell toed the common line and worshipped the Princess of Wales. She called her "my missus". Perhaps it was an exaggerated love.

> I do not think that I am quite sane upon that subject, and therefor hardly competent to write about it. It never occurs to me that she is a woman at all, but some exquisite little being being wafted straight from fairyland, to say and to do the kindest and prettiest things all the days of her life, and never, never to grow old and ugly, and be wafted back again some day from whence she came.[4]

In church Louise's eyes were glued on Alexandra. The Princess sat beneath a stained glass window and, when the sun shone, the colours poured upon her, enriching her with gold and glory. The royal children added to the spell—"Eddy", grave and quiet and ill-conditioned for life, George, so full of fun and mischief that he had to be restrained from playing his tricks during the service, the three little girls, anybody's girls, trilling "From Greenland's icy mountains". They crowded round their mother as if she was the only person in the world, and they called her "Motherdear".

This was a wring of the heart for Louise. She had lost a baby and the death of her husband had restricted her family to one. It would have been nice to have had five ponies at Appleton, a cluster of five to picnic with in the nut walk.

Sometimes the Princess would drive up to Appleton with her young ones for tea. The children would scamper off with Gerard to find eggs, climb stacks, hide in the hay and chase a rat. The two women were alone for a while. It was only then that the Princess relaxed. At "the Big House" she was always the hostess, always the wife of the Heir to the Throne. She was kind, understanding, human, but the aura was there. She played silly jokes and wild games and was not above pillow fights. But her bottom was not for pinching. In a trice she could envelop herself in the thick mantle of stateliness.

Louise's living room was a most relaxing place. There was always a bright fire, throwing racing shadows round the ceiling as the twilight came. There was a big round table, with a baize cloth over it and a polished brass oil lamp in the middle. She called the decoration "promiscuous". Among the assorted oils and engravings hung calendars old and new, from the cow cake merchants and the seedsmen and the medicinemen. On the bookshelves copies of the Royal Agricultural Journal and treatises on veterinary surgery alternated with the latest fiction and well worn volumes of poetry. On the sideboard Prize Cattle cards were propped up against fine old pieces of china. There were saucers of samples of wheat and barley and specimens of oil cake in amongst the plates of mince pies and soda cakes. There was a piano in the corner. There were bottles of home-made wine and a decanter of dark sherry and, by the fire, a toasting fork and a heap of logs and a hearthrug rich in dogs' hairs. Then the tea came in.

This was at five o'clock, after the men had finished work on the land and before milking time. Nanny brought in the blue Worcester tea-service and rounded up the children. There were muffins and home-made bread and strawberry jam and farm butter, and buns in little paper holders.

The Princess was most interested in the workings of Appleton farm and gave a helping hand by lending her royal patronage. Louise specialised in the County breed of cattle, Norfolk Polls, of blood-red colour and the darker the better. Little Princess Louise was allowed to be godmother to one heifer and to choose its name. To Louise's delight, it won First Prize at the Smithfield Club Show at the Agricultural Hall in London. As a reward, she presented the little Princess with a calf and in due season it also gained a First.

The Princess also took on the task of pig salesman and Appleton animals were to be seen on the royal farms of England,

Denmark and Greece. Louise went in for "Improved Norfolks", "little beauties, round balls with no noses to speak of, 'fit for a parlour' ". One went to the Princess's brother, King George of Greece, travelling on H.M.S. *Serapis* which took the Prince of Wales to India in the autumn of 1875. The pig, and other stock from Sandringham, were in the care of an old Norfolk cowman. The cowman's wife was "oneasy" at the thought of him crossing the ocean but he, although he had not been away from home before, took it all in his stride and as just one more job. On his return he reported to Louise: "He wouldn't a liked to a lived in them parts, but liked hisself very well there, and His Majesty were a very pleasant gentleman and uncommon pleased wi' the pig." Soon afterwards King Christian of Denmark came on a visit to Sandringham, sought out the cowman and asked for news of his son in Greece. "He's quite well, thank yer, sir, he ask after yer all, and he send his love to yer all, and he's quite well, thank yer."[5]

As regards beauty, Louise considered that Alexandra was peerless. At one time or another, she saw most of the queens of society and celebrated beauties of the day at Sandringham, "yet there was an indescribable something about her that threw them all into the shade".[6] The only near rivals were Lady Spencer, Lady Blandford and Lady Dudley. Louise had no time for the women whom she damned as "professionals"—on his return from India the Prince was fascinated in turn by Miss Chamberlain (an American whom the Princess dubbed "Miss Chamberpots"), Sarah Bernhardt and Lillie Langtry.[7] Beautiful they might be, but there was a quality of refinement missing, "though little they care for that so long as crowds follow them about, and Princes and Peers are in their train".[8]

Louise could not bear to see "her missus" deflated, written down. She had watched those professional beauties at the Sandringham balls, possessive, whispering, sure of themselves, guessing that if they had not already slept with the Prince, they most surely would. And Alexandra had to walk before them, acting, smiling, pretending, content only with the crumb that she knew, in Edward's heart, that he loved her best of all. Thank God for Oliver Montagu. His eyes were on the door, waiting for her to come in. She picked them up, beamed in on them, finding strength as from an electric wave. Always she danced the first after-supper waltz with him. The reason why Louise was so circumspect in her social contacts with the Prince was clear to see—Alexandra.

There was also the count of jealousy to be considered. Because

Louise had a child in the same age group as her own, the Princess was lavish with her invitations to birthday parties, or to watch fireworks and conjuring tricks. During the years that she was in favour, the Prince did the same. If he decided to have an impromptu dance, Louise was an obvious choice, communications being as they were. And it was this reason that she gave for her frequent appearances at "the Big House".

It is never worth while to arouse unnecessary irritation, and there is something in the vicinity of a court that excites an extraordinary restlessness in a neighbourhood, and an alarming development of the green-eyed monster. It seems as if I were always depreciating my own sex, but you do not see the best of them under those circumstances. I have noticed that women who are friendly and pleasant in a general way, will look black and queer, and make a tart remark or preserve an ominous silence, if you are incautious enough to name having been to a party to which they were not asked, while there are very few who would be glad that you went and enjoyed yourself, and frankly say that they would have liked to have gone too.[9]

The danger of dropping an incautious remark had constantly to be guarded against, for to Appleton came chance acquaintances whom Louise knew full well would not have sought her out but for her favoured position. The apparently innocuous remark over tea—"The Princess is not looking so well this year"—was in reality a lead to find out if she was going to have another baby. "Lady——— told us that the little Princess cried with fright at the conjuror the other evening" was a trap to discover whether Louise had been invited. If she confirmed or denied, she gave herself away. She was asked straight out if she was aware of the "under-current of vice" in the Prince's house, while another caller asked if the tales about him were true or false, as she would be glad to contradict them if they were not. It only needed a paragraph, quoting her name, to appear in some gossip column for Louise's goose to be cooked to a cinder. There was a real danger, for it was known that newspaper correspondents would pay five pounds for a description of the clothes which the Princess wore at a private party.

Fashions were news. Fashionwise, Alexandra was big news. The dull days of Victoria and Albert, when stout matrons ruled the Court and young ladies-in-waiting were firmly restricted, were gone. Victoria would have loved to have had a dress sense, but never did. She pirouetted before Lord Melbourne in a new frock, only to be told that it reminded him of an armchair cover. She was abominably dressed when she arrived in Paris for the state visit of 1855. She wore a plain straw bonnet and carried a parasol of glaring green. A white poodle was embroidered on her massive handbag.[10] In the 1870s she was tented in black and, when John Brown pointed out that a skirt had passed its heyday, she had it filed away, labelled with details as to the length and scope of its service.

The Empress Eugénie and Worth set Europe alight and then the slim Princess from Denmark, who had made her own clothes as a girl, grew up and took on the torch, becoming the most lovely clothes prop of them all.

She had an extraordinary gift. Whilst most beauties looked their best in a particular outfit, riding clothes, ball gown, tea dress, tweeds for the country, Alexandra came equal first in them all.

> You see her in full dress with rows of priceless pearls, and those magnificent diamonds which of all adornments are the most difficult to wear in profusion without exceeding the limits of good taste and not look smothered in them, and you think that decidedly evening dress sets her off to the best advantage. You see her in the morning and find you have made a mistake, and like her better in that quiet serge dress and her favourite Danish cross. Yes, most certainly she ought to be seen in the morning. Then in a bonnet, was there every anything like the Princess? And so on through all the changes. In her sailor's hat, or riding-habit, or rough ulster cap, driving the miniature four-in-hand of ponies that might have been Cinderella's in her fairy days, with silvery bells and dogs barking round, she is peerless.[11]

SOURCES

1   Cresswell, p. 146
2   Private information
3   Ponsonby: *Harry Ponsonby*, p. 359
4   Cresswell, p. 143
5   Ibid., pp. 194–5
6   Ibid., p. 185
7   Battiscombe: *Queen Alexandra*, p. 136
8   Cresswell, p. 185
9   Ibid., p. 182
10 Duff: *Victoria Travels*, p. 152
11 Cresswell, p. 185

17
War Again

By 1877 Louise was again feeling the cold wind of intrigue and accusation which had been hushed since the storms of ten years before. Mischief was in the air and irritations came her way. No longer did the Prince invite her to private parties and, in place of the jovial greeting to which she had been accustomed, she noticed, when she met him about the estate, that his "black" look was back once more. She could not understand why and many months were to pass before she found out.

The Prince wished to hire the shooting on a nearby estate, where the sport was very good. The owner of this estate was a close friend of Louise. He would not agree, proving adamant and forthright. The Prince could never bear to be crossed. If he wanted something, he would never accept that there might be a very good reason why he could not have it. If anybody "offended him personally, his private distaste affected his whole attitude towards the offender".[1] He was accustomed to having his own way in the "Prince-ridden" county and the refusal annoyed him. He looked about for a reason for the refusal, but without considering that he himself, his character and his reputation, might be the cause. His eye fell on Louise. Yes, it must be her! She had been blabbing to her friend about his shooting habits and moaning about the damage that the game did to her farm. She had not forgotten the old days and was out for revenge.

The Prince could never keep a grievance to himself and now he made his attitude clear to the lawyer and the agent. They were quick to take the hint. Although they had been most polite to Louise of late, both had scores to settle and wished to see a more amenable tenant at Appleton farm. Yet, in the event, the estate owner had never even mentioned the matter of the hiring to Louise. He just did not want the Prince, his entourage and his flock of fancy guests, parading about on his land.

The "insult", as the Prince deemed it, festered in his mind and became exaggerated out of all proportion. And now Louise's "old guard" of friends, men who had known the Prince since childhood and had influence with him, were no longer there to guide and counsel him. General Hall died in 1872, Charles Kingsley in 1875, and Sir Anthony de Rothschild in 1876. Bernal Osborne and Dean Wellesley were entering their last years. The Duke of Cambridge, at best a fairweather friend, was an infrequent visitor now. And, most telling of all, Mr Onslow, Rector of Sandringham, was ailing.

The Prince was ageing fast. At thirty-six he was thin on top and paunchy, well meriting his nickname of "Tum-Tum", and a coarseness had replaced the panache of youth. There was a significant change in his choice of feminine company. He was turning from the married women, older than himself, and feasting his hungry eyes upon the girls.[2] He was in financial difficulties. Although his annual income was over £100,000, he was over-spending at the rate of £20,000,[3] and the cause of the deficit was Sandringham. The capital that his canny father had accumulated for him was running out. He was turning also from the gay young men whom he had met during his Oxford and Cambridge days and seeking instead the company of rich and elder men who loved pleasure, "and among them the Prince discovered a special affinity with Jews".[4] In the event it was only natural that he should seek their company and advice, for the Dukes of Coburg had put much trust and confidence in the *Hof Jude*. Such a Bavarian Court Jew was now waiting in the wings—Baron Maurice de Hirsch. It was international magnates such as he who were to be the Prince's confidants and financial advisers for the next third of a century, although, in the field of money, the mare Perdita II was to prove of the greatest help.

The first round in the new battle scored a direct hit on Louise and wounded her severely. She was accused of causing the illness of Prince "Eddy". As she adored the royal children, her temper flared.

There was a chalk spring in Denbeck wood and the wood was on Louise's land. The Prince decided to tap the spring and provide Sandringham with an ample and pure water supply. The death of his father, followed ten years later by his own near escape from death, had imbued him with a dread fear of typhoid fever and, although his finances were in a precarious position, he decided to go ahead with the project. Accordingly in 1876 the work began.

The piping and the building of a pumping station and tower were a confounded nuisance to Louise. For months on end the contractor's men swarmed over her land and premises, and a new

road which she had built was cut to pieces by the carts bringing
bricks and pipes and machinery. The Prince was riding along it,
met Louise and expressed his annoyance at the ruts and holes. For
the only time he complained to her direct, apparently being under
the impression that it was *his* road and that she had cut it up "with
her usual malignity". She flashed back at him: "It is *my* road,
Sir, and your Royal Highness's carts have cut it all to pieces."[5]
He grunted and rode away.

Louise noted the importance to her landlord of his latest novelty
and improvement and accordingly was most circumspect. She
would not even allow a manure heap to be made until she had consulted the engineer in charge of the scheme.

At the beginning of July 1877 foundation stones for the ornate
water-tower were laid by the Princess, her youngest brother,
Prince Waldemar of Denmark, and Princes "Eddy" and George.[6]
Water was by this time flowing through the pipes to Sandringham
House. The Prince and Princess returned to London. On the 7th
news flashed round the estate that Prince "Eddy" had developed
typhoid fever.[7]

A few days later Mr Beck, the land-agent, arrived at Appleton.
He was in a "grand bustle". Without even saying "Good morning", he blurted out:

"Prince Albert Victor has typhoid fever and it's all your doing."

Louise just stared at him, too flabbergasted to speak.

"Yes," continued the agent, "Mr M—— has reported at Marlborough House that you allowed the farm drainage to poison the
water. I was up there on business and heard him tell the Prince
himself."[8]

When he had gone, she sat down, miserable, to consider the
import of the accusation. She did not as yet know how serious
the illness of the boy Prince was. Say he was to die! He was
second in line to the Throne. If the accusation stuck and spread,
she might be held responsible for killing a future King of Great
Britain. Then there was the attitude of the Princess to consider.
Would she ever come to tea at Appleton again?

She realised that she must take quick and positive action. She
knew Mr M—— slightly. He was "a gentleman about the Court"
and she had met him when visiting Sandringham. Straightway she
wrote to him, asking him point blank if it was true that he had
accused her of causing the young Prince's illness. She did not
mention the source of her information. She received from him a
most emphatic denial that he had done any such thing. No more
accusations were made. Louise was bewildered, but highly sus-

picious of the motives of Mr Edmund Beck. She was greatly relieved when the announcement was made on 28th July that Prince "Eddy" was well on the way to recovery.

Owing to the illness of Mr Onslow, she had been unable to turn to him for advice, as she had done on every case when she had been in trouble since his arrival at Sandringham twelve years before. Early in September her "knight and champion" died. "The loss to me was irreparable; I felt my doom was sealed."[9]

Louise sorely missed the Rector's strong and comforting arm on an afternoon in late October when farm men carried back to Appleton the limp form of her son. Gerard, just thirteen, had been allowed to join a shooting party. A gun went off by accident and he was severely wounded and in danger of losing his life. Louise drove him to Lynn, to the Bank House where her husband and daughter had died, so that he might be near to the doctors. She stayed with him, leaving the farm in the care of Mr Broome and the steward. She nursed him, never leaving his bedside until the crisis was over. Then, when tired out, she received a message that the Prince wished to shoot over the Appleton lands.

The Prince was down for his birthday battue—nothing was allowed to interfere with that. Among his guests were the Maharajah Dhuleep Singh and the Crown Prince of Hanover.[10] Louise dragged herself back to ensure that nothing interfered with His Royal Highness's pleasure. The horses were stabled, the traction engines driven back to the yard, the men ordered to stay about the farm buildings.

Now the men objected to the restriction. There was nothing they liked better than to watch the sport, mix with the beaters and maybe pick up a tip or pop a wounded bird into a capacious pocket. It was a welcome break in the stern and lonely routine of winter. As one said: "It would be wonderful lonely in the winter without the shooting and no one stirrin' about".[11] So Louise had to keep careful watch that none of them slipped behind a barn and disappeared.

That day Louise, weary and worried, must have been less stern and watchful than usual and one old labourer made good his escape. He got in the way between drives and the Prince spotted him from the hill. Down he strode, his party behind him, and in the farmyard of Appleton he halted before Louise. He then proceeded to anathematise her, tearing off strip after strip before the assembled guests, keepers and farm workers.

The Prince was in one of his tantrums. To his annoyance, his wife was away and he liked her to be present for his birthday party. She was at Abergeldie Castle, in Scotland, looking after her lady, Miss Knollys, who was ill. When she arrived at Sandringham and heard about the trouble, she did her best to make amends. Up to Appleton she trotted in the "Blues" cart and chatted before the fire. She listened to the tale of the shooting of young Gerard. And she said, in her inimitable way :

> What *did* you do? Only to think your precious boy to be shot! I cannot think what you *did* do![12]

But not even the tact and love of Alexandra could dam the torrent of selfishness of Albert Edward when in spate.

SOURCES

1   Benson : *King Edward VII*, p. 167
2   Battiscombe : *Queen Alexandra*, p. 173
3   Magnus : *King Edward the Seventh*, p. 121
4   Ibid., p. 141
5   Cresswell, p. 227
6   *Illustrated London News*, 7th July 1877
7   Ibid., 28th July 1877
8   Cresswell, p. 227
9   Ibid., p. 225
10   *Illustrated London News*, 17th November 1877
11   Cresswell : *Norfolk and the Squires, Clergy*, etc., p. 17
12   Cresswell, p. 226

18

No Money in the Bank

Depression came to agriculture. The high returns resulting from the Crimean and Franco-German wars began to drop, the fall being precipitated by the bad harvest of 1875, involving the country in a loss of £26,000,000. Two poor harvests followed, and there was but little improvement in 1878. The national loss rose to £80,000,000 and led to a depression, not only in agriculture, but also in commerce and trade.[1] A Royal Commission on the Agricultural Depression was appointed. On 28th March 1879 Disraeli, now Lord Beaconsfield, told the House of Lords:

> The remarkable feature of the present agricultural depression is this, that the agricultural interest is suffering from a succession of bad harvests, and that these bad harvests are accompanied for the first time by exceedingly low prices. That is a remarkable circumstance which has never before occurred, a circumstance which has never before been encountered. In old days, when we had a bad harvest, we had also the somewhat dismal compensation of higher prices. That is not the condition of the present; on the contrary, the harvests are bad, and the prices are lower.[2]

While the average price of English wheat from 1865–74 was 54 shillings, the average for the next decade fell to 46 shillings. By 1894 it was less than 23 shillings.

The summer of 1879 was wet and cold and the harvest a disaster. Farm after farm was thrown back on the landlords' hands and the newspapers were full of advertisements for holdings to let or for sale. The tenants could not pay the rents and the landlords were loath to make reductions. Farmers, being unable to appreciate what was happening and being unwilling, or incapable, of changing their methods, went to the wall, and there was no comfort in the prices obtained in the auction sales. The squires, finding themselves with untenanted farms, were faced with the alternative of letting the land lie derelict or farming it themselves. They were forced to sell their London houses, forego the social round and set about the task of keeping their country estates solvent. Their way of life was over, never to return. Many sold their estates, at low prices, their land falling into the hands of business men with international connections. Their difficulties were exacerbated by a constant pressure for higher wages. In 1871 the Trade Unions had extended their activities to include agricultural workers and attempted economies by a reduction in pay led to strikes.

The causes of the depression went far beyond the bad weather. The railways and the steamships had increased competition from abroad, depreciating the value of native produce. There had been enormous importation of corn and cattle. In the Middle West of America a vast new granary had begun to pour out a flood of grain, outstripping in supply the population increase. Then there was the question of gold. After the war of 1870, Germany began to form a gold reserve, switching £80,000,000 from silver. At the same time the production of the gold mines of Australia and California began to fall. The value of gold rocketed. As Lord Beaconsfield pointed out: "Gold is every day appreciating in value, and as it appreciates in value, the lower become prices."[3]

Louise, struggling alone to make ends meet on an isolated Norfolk farm, could not be expected to be fully conversant with the details of American production or to understand the repercussions of bullion transactions in Leipzig. But she could read only too clearly the sad story revealed by her account books. She showed them to a visiting north country friend. He shook his head and remarked that farming was "no trade at all".[4]

It was only natural that she should look for parochial causes for the troubles which were piling up about her. And there were plenty of those. The chief were labour and housing. The Prince's building programme was continuing unabated. He was very proud of the design of his new cottages and his rehousing scheme was earning him compliments from influential parliamentary figures. He said at a meeting of the Norfolk Agricultural Society at King's Lynn: "I live in a good house myself, and it is my wish that every labourer, when he returns home tired with his day's work, should have a comfortable home to go to."[5] This was most praiseworthy and superlative propaganda, but in the effect it did not apply to all labourers and quite naturally the obtaining of one of these havens of rest was high on the list of priorities of those who had not as yet been lucky. In the case of Louise's men, it was not a case of luck. There simply was no allocation for them.

Considering the extensive acreage that I held, a large proportion of the new model cottages ought to have been allotted to me; but they were not only given in other directions, but some of my men, whose houses had been pulled down, were turned out to live in any holes I could hire from cottage proprietors in the neighbourhood at an extra rent; whilst labourers who had been dismissed for misconduct (and they must have behaved badly indeed for me to turn them off) were given a good house or a good place in the Prince's service with higher pay and less work than I could afford to do.[6]

There was only one course open to her. Although there was an air of prosperity about Sandringham itself, outside the orbit of the Prince of Wales agriculture was in a parlous state and labour was readily available. So each morning, at first light, a waggon left Appleton for a village some distance away and returned with a gang of men. In the evening it took them home.

The days of even greater battues were beginning, the new landowners competing fiercely to produce the biggest bag. The Prince had shot widely on the Continent and returned with fresh ideas about game preservation and destruction. Ten thousand pheasants were bred annually at Sandringham and fed on grain. "Crack" shots became heroes and "duffers" were the butt of jokes round the dinner tables. The Prince was a good shot, but a showman and at best before a gallery. Unlike his son, George, who was more proficient and a true sportsman, he left the difficult birds alone. At lunch, in the big tent, the Prince would read out, before the ladies, the scores to date. The high scorers were applauded and fawned upon. When announcing a low figure, the Prince would pause and fix his eyes upon the "culprit" before revealing the degree of failure.

The proliferation of pheasants and hares coincided with the series of hard winters and Louise suffered damage to her root crops. She estimated this at some hundreds of pounds and accordingly claimed on the Prince's lawyer. She met him at the Audit in Lynn. He handed her a cheque for £50. She was forced to accept it as she was in debt and had a son's education to pay for. But she complained. She was told that the Prince must have his amusements and, if she did not like it, she must go. She replied that she had no objection to H.R.H. having his amusements, but that she could not afford to pay for them. The lawyer then lost his temper. He repeated all manner of stories that he had heard against her. Louise studied Edmund Beck, sitting at the same table. He was trying his utmost, by nudges and interjections, to restrain the lawyer. When he realised that Louise's cold and calculating eyes were upon him, he "betrayed himself by looking ready to sink through the floor with fright and confusion". But now Louise knew, without a shadow of doubt, who her enemy was.

There was a row. Mr Broome announced that he would not attend the Audit dinner unless the lawyer apologised to Mrs Cresswell. Knowing that he was at fault in losing his temper, he did so, most courteously. But the glove was down. Louise was after Edmund Beck.

The Prince gave her her chance. At a meet of the West Norfolk he spoke in a manner, both loud and rude, about the way the tenant of Appleton was letting down the land and neglecting her animals. He never could appreciate that Louise had many friends in the upper social strata. To him she was just a poor widow eking out a living by trying to farm, and, at face value, a subject for patronisation. The story of what the Prince had said was quickly in her hands. And as he had mentioned "disease", she knew full well where the story had originated. Flood water from the Sandringham land had overflowed on to one of her grazing meadows, causing casualties among her cattle. The agent, who was outwardly being most polite, had sent her his sympathy.

Next morning she drove up to the agent's house, marched in and, after repeating what the Prince had said, demanded how he dared to tell H.R.H. such a pack of lies. "He trembled all over, and in his terror, thinking I knew more than I did, let it all out. . . ."[7]

If ever a woman longed to be at a man with a hunting-whip, that woman was Louise Cresswell. That would have given him real grounds for complaint to his master. Instead, in her fury, she threatened an action for libel. The news spread quickly round the area and advice poured in upon Louise from all quarters. Some of it was suspect, some helpful, some just offered out of sympathy and kindness of heart. Others who had suffered at the hands of the agent hurried to tell her how they had dealt with the problem, each convinced that he had come out best. An old man had been accused of stealing a bell. In wrath he had written to the office, saying that "he were thankful he had never robbed the landlord of the smallest coin of the realm, much less steal a bell, and if he had done such a thing at his time of life, he'd deserve to have it hung round his neck to the end of his days with a great big placard to say how he come by it".

"What answer did you get?" asked Louise.

"Oh, honey and butter's nothen to it, nobody like me now,

don't know where I shall have to go to one day; Heaven ain't good enough for me, that's certain."[8]

She was given a "downright scolding" by the wife of one of the smaller Sandringham tenants.

> You don't know how to tackle that agent. Why, he treated my husband right shameful, and I went to him and I says, says I, "You'll make a rope here long enough to hang yourself on one of these days." He *was* angry and began to poke away at the fire. "No need for yew ever to poke a fire," says I, "it'll be poked hot enough for yew where yew'll go one day."[9]

The consensus of reasoned opinion was strongly against Louise resorting to law. If she did, it was argued, the Prince might go into the witness box on his agent's behalf. He had been in the box before and proved himself a polished performer. Or he might release a letter to the Press which would gain public sympathy. But it was when the enormous expense of a court duel was outlined to her that she finally decided not to proceed. Money was very short.

On a day in early summer of 1880 she attended the Tuesday market in Lynn and then called at the bank to collect the money to pay the wages. She was asked to go into the manager's office. There she was told, kindly but firmly, that the bank could make no more advances and that those which already had been made, were to be called in.

SOURCES

1   Ewald: *The Earl of Beaconsfield and His Times*, Vol. II, p. 476
2   Ibid.
3   Ibid., p. 479
4   Cresswell: *Norfolk and its Squires, Clergy*, etc., p. 14
5   Ibid., p. 36
6   Cresswell, pp. 228–9
7   Ibid., p. 234
8   Ibid., pp. 136–7
9   Ibid., 238

19
Curtain Fall

Louise was faced with the grim prospect of a forced sale at ruinous prices and of being torn from the home that she loved, the store house of memories of her husband and her children. She loved every Appleton field. She flinched from breaking faith with the small band of employees who had stuck by her through good times and bad, with her dogs and her horses and the cows which, when ill, she had nursed through the night by a lantern's light. "Where love has been there yet remains, an echo of the song that once it sang."

There was the boy's future to be considered. A conference of relations and close friends was held at the Bank House. The sadness of Louise was plain to see. As a result an offer was made to pay off the bank and provide sufficient capital for a fresh start. The sun shone again—but not for long. The benefactor was a business man and he stipulated that Louise's affairs be put on a business footing. The Sandringham authorities were to be approached and asked (a) to review the rent in view of the parlous state of agriculture, (b) to allot to Appleton a fair proportion of new houses, so that Louise might maintain a satisfactory labour force, and (c) that a written agreement should be entered into regarding reimbursement for damage caused by the ravages of game. The benefactor did not anticipate that there would be difficulty in obtaining agreement on all three points. As to the damage by game, when Gerard and Louise had entered the Appleton tenancy, there had only been a "gentleman's agreement", with assurances. But now the burden on tenants was widely appreciated and the Hares and Rabbits Bill was before Parliament. By proposing to give the occupiers of land "an unalienable concurrent right" to destroy ground game on their holdings, the new Government of Gladstone was making a bid for the tenant farmers' vote, although there was an honest desire to redress a grievance which had been long and urgently proclaimed.[1]

The reply of the Prince's lawyers came as a considerable shock. It was an emphatic—"No."

> Not one single concession would they make in game, rent, labour or anything that would enable me to accept this offer. They saw their opportunity and were down upon me with, "go, go, go", in all directions.[2]

There was no point in continuing to farm under the existing conditions. Losses were inevitable and sadly Louise rejected the kind offer of financial assistance. Meantime pressure was turned on to ensure that she did not change her mind.

Without giving prior notification of his arrival, a young and self-assured lawyer came to Appleton. He thus addressed Louise:

"I have been talking matters over with the Prince's lawyer and I advise you to go."

"Excuse me," she answered, "but have you been appointed the Prince's legal adviser for the district, or under his London solicitor? Who are you acting for?"

"For you."

"For me! By whose authority?"

It emerged that he had appointed himself, hoping, by stage-managing the exit of Louise, to ingratiate himself in influential quarters. Louise was, of course, to foot his bill. He left the farm hurriedly, the poorer by one return fare from London and the cab hire from Lynn. Louise had spoken, and he departed "with his possible vision of a Lord-Chancellorship considerably lessened".[3] He did not return.

The next move came from "the Big House". There the Princess was stamping her pretty foot and doing her best to save Louise. She informed her husband that she liked having Mrs Cresswell at Sandringham, and that she should not go and that something should be done. Under pressure, H.R.H. did something. It may have satisfied the Princess, who was a loving and peaceful woman, little concerned with the emancipation of women and their careers, but it certainly did not suit the proud and professional Mrs Cresswell. A secondary reason for the Prince's move was that he feared but one thing—public opinion.

His suggestion was that Louise should continue to live on the Sandringham estate, but should not farm. She was to send in her resignation, but she was not to mention in so doing that the reason was the damage done to her crops by game. Any other reason would do. She was to say that she placed her case "entirely in the Prince's hands". In return she was told that she might "expect the most liberal treatment". As for her son, the royal influence would be used to find him a suitable appointment as soon as he was old enough. A most doubtful enticement was that the agent would give her all help in preparing for the auction sale and in winding up her affairs, or, as she put it, "the 'understrapper' would rustle about in all directions to help in the sale and packing up, and I to say how good and kind everybody was!".[4]

Experience had taught Louise to mistrust the words "most liberal treatment",

> which I knew would not consist in coin of the realm, but in Royal invitations which I did not want, and in being pitchforked upon people who did not want me. Society women would be asked to take me up on the ground that they must be kind to poor Mrs Cresswell, to oblige the Prince.[5]

Louise did not want to be poor Mrs Cresswell. She did not want charity. She had no intention of becoming a royal toady. She simply wanted to be left alone to farm in her own way. She was an expert now, and she could have survived the depression. But she could not survive the depression combined with the whims of Albert Edward. She had no use for whitewash. When asked at the market why she was leaving the farm which she loved so well, she answered plainly: "Because I could not remain unless I killed down the Prince's game from Monday morning till Saturday night, and reserved Sunday for lecturing the Agent."[6]

The royal lawyer had sabotaged the resurrection offer of financial help; the Prince had put forward an unacceptable offer of charity, to satisfy his wife and to kill public sympathy for Louise should that eventuality arise. She was at the end of the road. She was finished.

> I had borne the burden and heat of the day, and, though the work was a pleasure, yet it was real work, and a severe mental and physical strain. I had not been cowardly, but fought my way through almost insuperable difficulties. And to be conquered at last! —I that prided myself, perhaps too much so, upon overcoming every obstacle, with a determination not to be crushed or defeated.[7]

The last nightmare months began. She was so rooted to the place, it seemed that the very fields would miss her. Now, with the perversity of nature, the sun shone brilliantly day after day. Seldom had the land looked better. The steam-plough tackle had done its job well and, as a visiting farmer remarked, it was like a garden. The men, sensing that an injustice had been done, were forthright in their condemnation of the "powers above" and worked without complaint when the weather broke once again. Volunteers offered their help and the steward was a jewel. Every head of stock had to be constantly watched for the slightest suspicion of disease. It was upon them that Louise depended for some financial return, the price of grain being as low as it was and machinery and implements a drug in the market. One week there was a rumour of "foot and mouth", but happily nothing came of it. This was her dread, for if disease came, she could neither keep nor sell the cattle.

It was her fellow farmers and the humble folk who backed Louise when help was most needed. She gathered their names in her heart and promised that she would come back to see them. A neighbour's wife entreated her:

> "Wherever you go or whatever become of yer, boast you were rew-ined by Royalty. Don't you forget now, rew-ined by Royalty, that'll help yer along like."[8]

On 18th September 1880 announcement of the sale, by a firm of Attleborough auctioneers, appeared in the local newspapers:

APPLETON HALL, SANDRINGHAM

Salter and Simpson are favoured with instructions from Mrs Gerard Creswell [sic] to sell on October 1st 1880 . . . dead and live farming stock . . . including inter alia . . . 24 horses . . . 88 head of neat stock . . . cows, bulls, calves, steers, weanings etc., etc., . . . 520 sheep . . . and 120 pigs of Mrs Gerard Creswell's improved Norfolk breed as sold to the Royal Farms of England, Denmark and Greece. . . .[9]

There followed a long list of farm tools and gear of all kinds.

Then the auctioneer was taken ill and total confusion reigned. There was nothing for it but for Louise to undertake the job of making up the lots herself. She felt like a judge determining execution day as she attached the numbers to stable, stall and sty. And, in contrast, she felt like some dull, stupid machine as, on the sale day, she watched her favourites knocked down to the hammer. This could not be reality, she thought.

There was an interval for lunch. She snapped back to her old self when she learned that the Prince's health was to be proposed. That went against the grain. But the healths of the Princess and her children were also to be drunk, so she agreed, as she wished to hear her "missus" cheered once more.

The sale dragged on towards the twilight. The steam-tackle,

which had cost hundreds and was as good as new, was knocked down for thirty pounds. The animals were led and driven away, to new homes or for slaughter. There was a farewell pat for a horse. The carts were loaded and rumbled off. The shouting of the drovers and the chatter of the loaders died away. Appleton lay dark and empty.

Louise checked the stalls and stables. The deadly silence was more overpowering and oppressive than any experience that she had ever endured. The loneliness was past description.

There had ever been an undersong from the farm, faint music to which she had become so accustomed that she hardly realised it was there until it had gone. It was the music of many animals, moving, grunting, making their own noises, rubbing against a door, rattling at a manger, scrubbing out a feeding trough. A dog barking at a fox, a cock telling of the dawn. She who had never been frightened, was frightened now. She turned towards her bed with hate in her heart. "Verily there are things far worse than murder; and to leave you your bare life, after taking away all that makes life worth having, is a far more flagrant breach of the Sixth Commandment."

The agony was not over yet. The following week her household effects were to be sold. She had decided that, for the future, the only thing that she could do was to travel about the world for a while. She had been lent some rooms in Lynn in which she could store her more precious possessions, but the rest had to go. Now came the awful decision—what to keep and what to sell.

Memory's label was tied to all her possessions. Every piece recalled some face, some moment in time. There were wedding presents, and purchases made with Gerard, and bargains picked up at auction sales.

> The nurseries were the worst part, for everyone who has lost one child, and has only one left, knows how dear a relic becomes. There lay everything they have used and played with, and where my happiest hours had been spent.[10]

Just as Queen Victoria had done in the case of Albert, leaving his possessions as they were when he died, his pen upon the blotter, his walking stick propped in the corner, his hat upon the peg, so had Louise left her drawing-room untouched since the day that her husband died. They had arranged it together, and so it had stayed through the years. Now she had to disturb the ghost of him. There was the picture of herself which the Princess had

146

given them soon after they came to Appleton. As she took it from the wall and placed it carefully in the packing case, it seemed to Louise as if she was placing it in a grave. She moved to the piano and played a tune which she and her husband had loved. The notes echoed back to her from all the empty rooms above and she slammed down the lid in terror.

There was a crumb of comfort for her on the sale day. She noticed that the local people, some of whom she knew well and some only by sight, were buying up all the lots. The strangers who had come in search of bargains were looking most put out. She guessed that, if she ever came back to Sandringham, she would see most of her treasures again.

Only a few hours left now. The house was empty but for the personal luggage standing drearily in the empty hall. The servants were spending the night in a neighbouring village. Only Nanny was with Louise.

There came the clatter of hooves on the drive and the Princess arrived with her lady. She was in her gay four-pony carriage and she drove herself. They talked a little while. Louise had always taken her "missus" to the door and waved her away. She could not do this now, see her drive out of her life. She sat, head bent, on the one remaining chair. The Princess said her goodbyes and went to her carriage. Then she sent her lady in with a message —"Tell her I *am* so sorry for her, so *very* sorry."[11]

It was raining and the autumn leaves falling from the trees were Appleton's tears at parting. The cab from Lynn was waiting at the door, its driver crouched on the box, a rug across the horse. Louise did not know how long she sat there, for she had not the strength to snap the link of time. It was getting dark. "We must go now," said Nanny, and took her arm.

> I never wanted to go away. If obliged now and then to take an entire rest, I was homesick and in a fidget to get back the whole time, and thought there was nothing in the world so beautiful as Appleton when I turned the corner of the hill and looked down upon it in the valley beneath, quite impatient for the welcome at the front door; and that would be reflected . . . in the fresh muslin curtains and flowers in my room, the dogs almost tearing me down, and the greeting of the animals on my rounds. It was worth going away for the pleasure of returning.[12]

This time there was to be no return.

SOURCES

1   *The Graphic,* 12th June 1880
2   Cresswell, p. 231
3   Ibid., p. 233
4   Ibid., p. 231
5   Ibid.
6   Ibid., p. 232
7   Ibid., p. 234
8   Ibid., p. 238
9   *Lynn News and County Press*
10 Cresswell, p. 241
11 Ibid., p. 237
12 Ibid., p. 111

20

Aftermath

The departure of a broken-hearted woman struck no chords of mercy in the hearts of either the Prince or his agent. To them, it was good riddance to an awkward bitch. At Sandringham, not to bend the knee to Albert Edward was unforgivable.

Louise had been defiant to the last. Anger was the antidote to sadness and courage was the quality which she admired most. She had "said a great many things that I regret, and done a great many that I deplore".[1] She left no margin for neutrality and Beck made note of those who rallied to her aid. Partisanship was strong in the conversation round the dinner tables of Norfolk and at many the subject of "poor Mrs Cresswell" was made taboo. But, for Edmund Beck, a flag of victory fluttered over Appleton.

Louise entrusted the winding up of her affairs to her old friend and adviser, Mr Broome, who had come in at the beginning of her story when he had taught Gerard how to farm twenty years before. He prided himself upon never being taken-in upon business matters, but, when the task was over, he declared that he had been "done" for the first time in his life. The entire hay and turnip crop was seized to make up a balance of unpaid rent. A valuer's assessment of the amount due to Louise was waved on one side. It totalled £2,640. All Mr Broome could extract was "a few hundreds . . . and a few more added on and insultingly called 'a present' ".[2] The Prince seemed to think that money given as a "present" had an inflated value, as if the coins could be sold at a high price as souvenirs from the royal pocket.

Bitter, Louise took ship for America. As she stood by the rail, the pictures of Appleton in her mind were reflected in the grey water of the Atlantic. The years that were gone passed in procession through her dreams at night. She posed problems, asking herself, over and over again, if she had managed differently, or taken drastic action, would the final outcome have been changed? She could find no solution to the flood of misfortunes which had overtaken her since 1875. Only if her champions—Lake Onslow and Charles Kingsley, Anthony de Rothschild, Dean Wellesley and General Hall—had lived, could she have survived.

She travelled widely, from one wild frontier to another. She found peace in the prairies and ranches of the Far West, returning to her normal self when she was among horses and cattle again. She decided that there would be one more round in the Appleton contest. She had been near to being counted out in the last, but now she was back on her feet and determined to win. She began to write the story of her eighteen years on the Sandringham estate.

She returned to England in 1886. She put up at an inn not far from Sandringham. She drove round the villages that she had known so well and she was hugged at cottage doors. "I was almost dragged into the house, and feasted upon new bread and butter, ham, and cake, until I begged for mercy, the news-telling chatter being interspersed with, 'To think I should ever see yure again; I *am* pleased'." She saw again the pictures and the ornaments and the vases which once had belonged to Appleton. She heard how the new tenant there had been granted all the advantages for which she had craved, new houses among them. She heard how those who had befriended her had suffered at the hands of the agent, and she called upon them. The love that she found made her feel that there was something in life still worth living for. She heard that there was a rumour that she was writing a book and that some at "the Big House" were worried.

The book was published the following year. It was believed that part of it was "cut" by the publisher. It was rushed out before Louise had time to make the proof corrections. Too quick for Edmund Beck. He managed to buy up the majority, but he could not stop copies reaching the libraries and many a Norfolk bookshelf held one, discreetly tucked away. The last round went to Louise.

Louise Mary Cresswell died at Abilene, Texas, on 2nd July 1916. She was eighty-six-years old. Her body was exhumed and brought to England by Wells Fargo. It was buried at North Runcton on 16th November.[3]

And as for Appleton, Louise's successor stayed for but a few years, thereafter the farm land being merged with the royal estate and being directly administered. Major-General Stanley Clarke, the Prince's equerry, lived there for a time. When, in 1895, Princess Maud became engaged to Prince Charles of Denmark, the Prince of Wales gave Appleton to his daughter. He wished her to have a foothold in England and stipulated that she visit it at least once a year.[4] He supervised the improvements himself, making many interior alterations, including the installation of central heating.[5] An army of gardeners transformed the homely garden which Louise had made and away went the sixteenth century Paston gateway and dovecot.[6] In time a castellated extension was added. Another change came in title. The house had for long been known as Appleton Hall, although only the foundations of the Paston building remained. Now it became Appleton House, thus bringing it into line with Sandringham which, before the arrival of the Prince, had also been a Hall.

After their marriage in 1896 Prince Charles and Princess Maud made Appleton their home and there their only child, Olaf,* was born in 1903. Two years later they became King Haakon and Queen Maud of Norway. Queen Maud loved her Norfolk home. She had known it ever since she could remember, associating it with cream teas and Louise and young Gerard and games in the farmyard. She continued to visit it throughout her life, sometimes as often as three or four times a year, which was too often for the liking of some Norwegians. In 1929 Crown Prince Olaf spent part of his honeymoon there. Queen Maud died in a London nursing home on 20th November 1938, on the same day of the same month as had her mother thirteen years before. Hilde Marchant wrote:

> The royal standard of the House of Norway dropped to half-mast on a country house in Norfolk today. This gabled, Victorian mansion was a royal residence, for though Queen Maud of Norway had a palace and a throne in Norway, her home was Appleton House, Sandringham. . . . Her obituary should be written by Hubbard, the gardener. . . . He worked for Queen Maud for forty years, and saw her when she was happiest. Here she was the lady of the house and, by coincidence, a queen. "She was a lovely woman," he said. "This was her real home, she loved this place."[7]

The next lovely lady to put her touch on Appleton House was also a Queen—Elizabeth, now Her Majesty Queen Elizabeth the Queen Mother. In 1940 "the Big House" was closed for reasons of economy and when the Royal Family sought respite from the strain of war they stayed at Louise's old home. There was an echo of her to be found in the Queen's transport. Petrol being short, she drove around the estate in a pony cart, just as Louise had done. But there was a contrast in vehicles. While the Queen's was neat and sedate, Louise's could lay claim to neither.

* Now King Olaf of Norway.

The trap I drove about in, "Agricultural Distress", hadn't its equal in the countryside. It had been patched and mended by local talent until there was hardly any of the original structure left. Sometimes a wheel would fly off, or a shaft snap in two; once it collapsed through the bottom coming out, and, when too rotten to hold a nail, was tied up with rope. The harness was not so bad, for my "screws" were not always of the quietest, and had there been time for broken bones, I might have had a plentiful crop. When they were too obstreperous, I steered into the nearest ploughed field which soon took it out of them.[8]

Famous people came to Appleton and great events were decided in the room where once Louise had worked on her accounts. The climax in its story came in the form of a telephone call. It was from Mr Winston Churchill to King George VI. The message was that the war in Europe was drawing to its close.[9] It was at Sandringham House that the Royal Family gathered at Christmas, 1945.

There were to be no more mistresses for Appleton. A farming widow and two Queens had graced its eighty years. While, since the days of war, the farm has become a show piece, the house has slept behind the shrubs and trees. It is sad now, sad as the day when weeping Louise left it, in the rain, for ever. The ghost of her lies safe behind the wide hedge of thistles and nettles. Perhaps it has become hers again. In the spring the green leaves come back to the nut trees.

SOURCES

1 Cresswell, p. 236
2 Ibid., p. 244
3 North Runcton Church Records
4 *Daily Express*, 21st November 1938
5 *The Graphic*, 29th July 1896; *The Queen*, 25th July 1896
6 Cathcart: *Sandringham*, p. 139
7 *Daily Express*, 21st November 1938
8 Cresswell, pp. 119–20
9 Duff: *Elizabeth of Glamis*, p. 254

Appendix
Louise Cresswell's Farming Diary

When friends came to tea at Appleton farm on the summer Sunday afternoons, sat cool behind the curtains of vines which draped the bay windows, heard the soft lowing and bea-ing and the munching of the cows and the sheep, they thought my life must be one unbroken bliss. It used to be—"How I should like to have a farm!" and "How delightful it must be to lead a life like this!" I don't know if they would have liked it "all round", for they must soon have found out that it was not all cakes and cream. But I would not have led any other life for the world. I found that the *bona-fide* farm "worrits" were bearable and had nothing of the petty galling nature about them that embitters so many women's lives. Cattle diseases, strikes, free trade and other "burning questions" you share with the rest of the agricultural world, and have a wide horizon for your cares instead of a narrow, carking one. And supposing I was a little overworked and overdone sometimes out of doors, all was rest and peace within. The house-keeping had been handed over to the nurse and, while other servants came and went, wanting a "change", she stayed on for ever and would do anything for us; the governess wrote the letters and did the flowers and refinements, and the child completed the party. I indeed grudged the days as they passed.

There was the endless variety of farm life, for each season brings its excitement and change of occupation. The spring is the most important time—heaps of work crowding in together, seed sowing and lambing time in one. A flock is so profitable that you must put up with the trouble; but imagine between five and six hundred lambs arriving in quick succession, and the previous care and watching, for the ewes must not eat this or that, or be turned upon land that disagrees—one part of a field will disagree with them and the rest be perfectly healthy—and your shepherd, if he is worth anything and attached to his charge, will be the very plague of your life, for if anything goes wrong he declares it is because "his ewes" (he never condescends to calls them "yours") "worn't allowed to have that there bit of 'olland or new-ley that would just a suited 'em to that there stack of hay".

Shepherds always seem to grudge the other animals everything they eat, whether the sheep want it or not, and would like to roam all over the place, and on to your neighbours' as well, and then would not be satisfied. When you shut up a piece of hay they are hankering after it all the time and, if you are weak enough to give in and run short at lambing time, they will declare "they would a done without it, and a pretty predicament we're in now!" I suppose the restlessness of the sheep is infectious, and to decide how far you should give in or hold out is one of the most difficult tasks you have. It was a great relief when the last ewe and her progeny walked out of the lambing-yard—a nursery that is fitted up in a sheltered place—and the shepherd, who is encamped for the time in a moveable house on wheels, goes back to his cottage, and washes and shaves, an operation that is a superstition with the old fashioned ones not to perform during the camping out.

Sowing the spring crops is of equal importance, though not so risky and distracting. The cultivation of barley comes by intuition to the Norfolkers and, with the fear of Bass and Allsop before them, who will have a perfect sample or go elsewhere, they have become masters of the art in which they may be equalled but not surpassed. You know that the land must be highly pulverised, but not too highly manured or the crop will "lodge", that if sown too soon the frost will catch it, or if too late it won't "tiller". You welcome the biting wind which chills you to the bone, for does it not produce "the peck of dust worth a king's ransom"? You would be glad to keep on sowing day and night if you could, for every hour is of consequence. You must have relays of horses and keep the drill going all through the noon-time. The extra wages are worth paying, for, if you don't seize the chance when it comes, you may not get it again that year.

Oats are much easier to grow but quite a secondary considera-tion. They are put in either before or after barley when there is a break in the favourable weather.

After barley and oats come mangolds and turnips and, when everything is up, there is the excitement and interest in seeing them grow and watching the effect of different manures and soils. In summer the "haysel" is the great occupation, and then the "turnip-hoeing and scouring", and so on till harvest.

From May to October the stocks are shifted backwards and forwards to the marshes, a long strip of land that makes a ribbon border to the coast. Slices of it are parcelled out among the upland corn farms where grass is scarce. They are wild, dreary flats when you are down among them, with broad dykes for drainage, and banks for keeping out the tide and defining the boundaries.

A haystalk looks colossal, a figure walking on the bank a giant and a bullock standing out against the sky, Brobdingnagian. That "low leaden line beyond" is the Wash and that "savage lair" in the distance is the German Ocean. There is a weird picturesqueness, and queer sounds and echoes, that you see and hear nowhere else. The autumn skies and sunsets are magnificent. Nature is full of compensations and, if you want scenery in the Eastern Counties, you must look up instead of down. With a little imagination you will discover Alpine peaks and mountains and Turneresque colouring to your heart's content.

Creeks, ending in miniature harbours, wind in and out of the marshes and, wherever there is a creek, there you will find a village. But who built those cathedral-sized churches, and where the population came from who attended them, I leave to the archaeologists to explain. The villages are noted smuggling resorts, and you may still see lonesome public-houses and outlying farm premises suspiciously near the harbours, where the horses would be found in the early morning reeking from some midnight expedition—and no questions asked. There may be one or two prosperous farmers of whom you will hear that "they made their money in them smuggling times", or "they broke up a rare smuggling lot on his place once upon a time, but he'd taken good care of hisself afore it were found out".

In October the young horses and bullocks were brought back from the marsh and settled in their winter quarters. The working teams were always at home, but never allowed to be stabled excepting for grooming and feeding. In summer they were turned out to grass at night, and in the winter into well littered yards, which makes them less liable to chills than if brought straight out of a steaming stable.

The forward bullocks were picked out early in the winter, for fattening in the boxes: they get on so much better under cover and in separate compartments where they can't prod one another or fight over the food. There was a pathway between the boxes, roofed overhead like a sort of Burlington Arcade, only much more interesting. It was a splendid place for walking up and down in the winter, or for a Sunday afternoon lounge, and not at all cold if you sat on a heap of straw, with the bullocks all around.

Beyond the boxes, and opening into them, were the turnip and chaff, engine, meal and cake houses. The cake was generally bought by contract in the summer when it was cheaper, as it was delivered as "back carriage" for the corn. We had fixed up some very useful machinery, which turned two small mills for cake and meal on one side and cut the straw and hay into chaff on the other. These fell through troughs into their respective compartments below, were mixed together and given to the bullocks with sliced turnips—the equivalent of meat, bread and vegetables. Sometimes four to five hundred sheep were fattening at once which, with the bullocks, ewes and lambs, and a handful for the young stock, made the cake bill mount up into the four figures. I regulated the quantity for each lot and, when it was to be increased, I checked it off against the cake in store.

Trundle, the yardman, weighed it out. He also fed the home stock, milked, brought up calves, poultry and pigs, and did sundry other work with the necessary assistance. It was a very important post and I think that I had the best man in the county. He could neither read nor write, and his thoughts were concentrated on his work. He was kind and clever with the animals and did not mind what trouble he took or how often he sat up at night when there was an invalid. "Trusty" Trundle I might have called him, for he was a faithful servant who stayed with me to the end. He was "my man" as, although the steward would give a hand in the yards if wanted, he had quite enough to do on the land, and I preferred keeping the management of the stock entirely in my own hands.

The days of the week brought as much change as the seasons, with special meaning attached to Mondays, Tuesdays and Sundays. On Monday morning the dealers were on their rounds and there was generally something to sell in a large or small way. After the North Country buyers began to frequent Lynn market, and good auctions and salesmen were established, I sent the best lots there to be sold, glad to get rid of the bargaining at home, higgling half the morning over sixpences. But as sixpence a head when selling two hundred sheep is five pounds, you must stand out for it and not think about the trouble.

Tuesday was market day and then nearly all the countryside, gentle and simple, flocked into Lynn for business, gossip and shopping. In place of the comparative silence reigning in the old town during the rest of the week, the pavements were blocked with people chattering in broad Norfolk and relating the latest news and grievances with an "I says and she says" and "I says, says I". The county people and the clergy attending Tuesday market were invited to luncheon at the Bank, while the rest of the community made for the Market "ordinaries"* of various grades and prices.

I did not go in for the Bank luncheons every Tuesday, although I enjoyed a business excuse for an outing and a gossip. If I had done so, a certain section of my labourers would have turned it into a pilfering and loitering day. One Tuesday, when they thought I was safely off to Lynn, I found a man helping himself to the engine coals. He was so busy filling his sack that it was not until he turned round to hoist it on to his shoulder that he discovered that I had been watching him all the time.

This petty thieving is a great nuisance, both to oneself and the honest ones, who don't like to see it and don't like to tell, and there are so many things on a farm that cannot always be put away. They would not commit a burglary, but will lay hands on odds and ends of "portable property". If they keep pigs or poultry, you may find that they are fattened at your expense and certain carts travelling along the high road are very convenient for popping things into. Not that they consider it a very grave offence. "Getting into trouble" is their word for being caught in abstracting your goods, in the same style that the contraband village babies are called "misfortunes".

Sunday was a real day of rest, and one must lead a full working life to know what that means. We spent the summer afternoons in the nut walk and had nursery tea in the shade, the governess, nanny, myself and the boy, with the dogs lying peaceful about us. Everything was so reposeful and different to other days, the animals feeling it as well as ourselves. Although Trundle was obliged to come up for feeding and milking, he wore his semi-Sunday clothes and looked like Sunday. From where we lazed we could see the public footpath crossing the little piece of park left over from the Paston Domain. Along this the villagers walked in their Sunday best, the young children picking flowers and playing with their dogs, the elder girls, upgraded to "virgins", casting demure glances at the shy young men. Along the path and back again, the parties greeting one another with old world courtesy. Then the music of the church bells came up from the valley, merging with the hum of the insects.

In contrast there were the "casualty" days, when pressure of work and catastrophes crowded in all at once. The following is a specimen.

* Eating-houses.

Five o'clock—looked out to see if it would be fine enough for haymaking later on. Six—talked over the hay with the steward and went round the yards. Seven—in the milking sheds, came in for a time and dressed for riding. Eight—rode round with the steward inspecting everything. Ten—had breakfast and was comfortably settled to *The Times* when Trundle came up to say that a cow "warn't right". Went out at once and stayed a long time watching and attending to her. Finding it likely to be a serious case of fever, sent for the Veterinary. Spent a great part of the afternoon with the invalid and then went into the hay field.

Towards evening the cow became much worse, dashing herself about, and would have been delirious if she had been a human being. Another man was called in to help. During the scrimmage a second cow became indisposed. Took disinfecting precautions, but was obliged to spare Trundle to look after her. Under his care she did very well.

Ordered supper for the men and something for them to eat during the night. Settled the work for the next day with the steward and back again to the "hospital". After impressing upon Trundle that he was to come and "hallow out" under my window if there was a change for the worse, fell into the sleep, not of the faithful, but of the exhausted. The cow pulled through, but it was the worst case that I ever attended. The remedies that I used were sedative medicines, whisky gruel, mustard rubbed down the spine, and the head bathed constantly with the coldest water. There was also a favourite prescription of mine that hardly ever failed to give relief—a blanket dipped in water as hot as she could bear, wrapped round the cow, and rugs put over her to keep the steam in.

When there was a crisis among the animals and the men were staying with them, I would go in and out to see how they were getting on. Even then, there would be compensation. On a summer or a frosty winter night, the moon was so beautiful shining over the old ruined church and tower, as I walked through long shadows, in the intense stillness, to the cattle sheds or stables.

The evenings were the most solitary time, particularly after my boy went away to school. One winter I tried music, but it sounded so uncanny in the emptiness that I gave it up and studied veterinary surgery and agricultural chemistry instead. Then there were the accounts, which took a long time, for the pages would not add up twice alike. But with good fires and plenty of light, it was never dull. I don't think solitude ever is. The real trial in life is an uncongenial or "nagging" relative or companion, and that I took good care to avoid. Once a Scottish kinswoman of my husband's, a well known lady traveller, turned up to enliven me with a visit. She declared that she delighted in it all and found it less like civilisation than anything she had met since returning from the Himalayas.

The front door was a worry. It was a weak affair, opening down the middle, with a lock that never went right. Then the village lunatic took a fancy to breaking into Appleton, and the staff was at the other end of the house. He was very powerful, and dangerous at times, and one evening I only kept him at bay by fetching my gun and threatening to shoot him. The next night the wind howled and tattered round the house as if there were eight corners of the compass instead of four. I listened and was on my guard. The door burst in and there was a sound as if a troop of people were sweeping down the passage and into the hall. I was cut off! It turned out that the force of the hurricane had proved too much for the lock, but I had had enough. I sent for the lunatic's son-in-law and insisted that he be kept at home. The son-in-law agreed that the lunatic "hadn't ought to be prowling about, but the trewth were he were made up o'nothen but wickedness, and had been that troublesome they was obliged to turn him out o'doors". The "that troublesome" consisted in his having concealed a pitchfork in the house and suddenly attacking the family with it! It seemed nobody's place to send him to an asylum. At last he took up his abode in a hole which he had burrowed on the heath and furnished it with a boiler and saucepan stolen from a neighbour's kitchen. The policeman being called in, he was removed to where he ought to have been sent long before.

But before he was taken away, we had another scare. At eight o'clock one night the front door bell rang loudly. We never had "front door" callers at that time. It was unheard of in that isolated place. I came from my room. The staff emerged from their quarters and gathered in the hall. Among them was the man who drove the brougham. We looked at one another. The bell rang again. I advanced towards the door, followed at a discreet, and considerable, distance by the staff. It was apparently considered that it was the Missus's place to go first at all times! The caller came from the Princess of Wales, with the message that there was to be a conjuring party that evening for the royal children and that Gerard's invitation had been overlooked.

As an occupation for the lonely evenings I had a class for the boys who worked on the farm, Gerard helping to teach them.

I suppose they liked it or they would not have walked down from the village through slush or snow. No constraint was put upon them to come, and they had nothing but a piece of bread and cheese before they went home. Even the under gamekeeper's boys asked to join. Most of them had learned something before, but one or two were in a state of deplorable heathenism, had never heard of Noah and the Ark, or Joseph and his brethren, and looked as if I had just discovered the facts for their amusement. There was the usual sharp, forward boy who wants to answer all the questions and let none of the others speak; and the shy, quiet boy, who knows quite as much or more, only it has to be dragged out of him; the *Morning Chronicle* boy who is burning to tell you the news of the village; and the Ranter boy whose only notion of religion is "fire and brimstone, please ma'am." They behaved very well, took it as a company-mannered occasion, and reserved their troublesome ways for the farm. But even there I liked the "them boys" element. After Gerard went to school, they looked forward to the holidays as the treat of the year. We got up a cricket team of all ages and sizes and wound up with a supper at the end of the time.

With this new education craze I suppose another race of juveniles will be turned out, destitute of manners, religion, and no respecters of persons. And pretty useless they will be for agricultural purposes, shut up in those hot schoolrooms for years, and idling about the village between times, their brains crammed with all sorts of rubbish, rendering them mentally and physically unfit for their work. They will not know a plant from a weed, and be tumbling off horses and stacks, and prodding one another with the forks, and cutting their legs to pieces with the scythes, which cannot be learned "how not to do" upon scientific principles, but only by practice and experience. Nine or ten years old is the latest at which they ought to make a beginning. They can pick up quite enough book learning by that time and keep it up at the evening school, and religion on Sundays.

I had an old neighbour who was known as the "Last of the Norfolk Farmers". He was a travelled man and had been to Rome, but was reticent over that part of his life and I think would have preferred to boast that he had never been out of Norfolk. The new style of estate management was not all to his liking, having been accustomed to transact business with the "Barrownite" or "Squire" himself. He came across to help in emergencies and gave valuable advice, until he began to treat me as an agricultural pupil and "blow me up" for mistakes.

"Whatever ere you after in that there field?" I explained. "That's all right. I were just a goin' to give it yer."

His "giving" generally took the form of rich cakes and fruit for Gerard, sent up in baskets with the whitest of cloths, and polite little three-cornered notes in beautiful Norfolk, to request the acceptance, &c. When riding round his farm he said that he "could see us, and when we was riden round we could see him". I don't know if we were worth looking at, but am sure he was. He was a sight to behold setting off on market day with his housekeeper in a high vehicle of ancient build, and costume to match—beaver hat with broad buckle and band, wide expanse of shirt front and frills, ponderous chain and seal, and spotless top boots.

He was generous with his advice when the most important dates on my calendar came round—the cattle shows. These were my field days, particularly the London ones where you have the opportunity of professional discussions with agriculturists from all parts of the world, and afternoon teas with your private friends on the straw in your own compartment.

My aspiration for show honours only began to be realised after years of preparation, as I could not give fancy prices for any particular strain and was obliged to go to work in the least expensive way. I should have liked to go in for Shorthorns, like the celebrated Lady Piggott. But if she could afford to have a cow of three thousand pounds on her mind, I could not, and had to content myself with the breed of the County, the Norfolk Polls. My great rival was a well known Norwich manufacturer who could buy up anything he liked and I almost despaired of getting beyond a Second Prize until, one winter at the Smithfield Club Show, the hour of triumph came with a decided First.

If you get a First Prize, it ought to pay expenses, besides giving you a good name in the agricultural world. But only the initiated would believe the petting up and handling they require from the first. You pick out the most promising looking calves, likely to grow into good looks, which a breeder's eye soon detects. They must not go back for a day, or lose the "bloom", or be kept too hot or too cold, while the appetite and digestion are carefully studied and pampered. This goes on for two or three years, exhibiting them meanwhile in graduated classes, for which they have to be gentled and broken in like colts, or they would not be led out with proper dignity before the Judges. And the finishing touches, up to the last moment! I will not betray the secrets of my trade and relate how those exquisite coats are doctored up, but dressing a girl for a ball is not half the time and trouble.

A prize makes up for everything when the awful moment is over, after your fate has been trembling in the balance, perhaps the Judges differing and an umpire called in. Then the rosette is tied on and the congratulations come pouring in. You can tell by the herdsmen's faces which are the prize winners without looking at the cards. But a week is too long for the animals, the herdsmen and yourself, and, if you have brought the yardman up, you are in a fidget to send him back again. It is like taking the nurse away and leaving the children at home with the nursery-maid.

I also took prizes for cart horses, but I generally sold the very promising ones, thus avoiding a possible future of spavins and sprains and other ills that horse-flesh is heir to. If you refuse a good price, something is sure to happen soon afterwards. I had thought of thoroughbreds at one time, but my old neighbour warned me that "if I went into that line, I should want no executors"— the Norfolk way of explaining that I would have nothing to leave when I died. What a delight it would be to be able to farm regardless of expense and insensible to profit or loss! Anyone can farm if they have the money, but the difficulty is to make it pay.

Bibliography

ANON. *King Edward the Seventh*. Nelson. 1911.

ANON. *Sandringham—A Guide to the Grounds*. Estate Office. 1973.

ANON. *Uncensored Recollections*. Nash & Grayson. 1924.

ANTRIM, Louisa, Countess of. *Recollections*. King's Stone Press. 1937.

ARTHUR, Sir George. *Concerning Queen Victoria and Her Son*. Hale. 1943.

ARTHUR, Sir George. *Not Worth Reading*. Longmans Green. 1938.

ASHTON, Rev. Patrick. *Sandringham Church*. Pitkin Pictorial.

BAILEY, John (Ed.). *The Diary of Lady Frederick Cavendish*. 2 vols. Murray. 1927.

BALDWIN SMITH, Lacey. *Henry VIII: The Mask of Royalty*. Cape. 1971.

BARNETT SMITH, G. *The Life of Queen Victoria*. Routledge. 1897.

BATTERSEA, Constance. *Reminiscences*. Macmillan. 1922.

BATTISCOMBE, Georgina. *Queen Alexandra*. Constable. 1969.

BENSON, A. C. (Ed.). *The Letters of Queen Victoria, 1837–61*. Murray. 1907.

BENSON, E. F. *As We Were*. Longmans Green. 1932.

BENSON, E. F. *King Edward VII*. Longmans Green. 1933.

BLOMEFIELD, F. and PARKIN, C. *History of Norfolk*. 1805–10.

BOLITHO, Hector. *Victoria The Widow and Her Son*. Appleton-Century. 1934.

BROADLEY, A. M. *The Boyhood of a Great King*. Harper. 1906.

BUCKLE, G. E. (Ed.). *The Letters of Queen Victoria, 1862–1901*. Murray. 1926–32.

BUXTON, Aubrey. *The King in His Country*. Longmans Green. 1955.

CATHCART, Helen. *Sandringham*. W. H. Allen. 1964.

CECIL, David. *Lord M*. Constable. 1954.

CLIVE, Mary. *This Sun of York*. Macmillan. 1973.

COHEN, Lucy. *Lady de Rothschild and Her Daughters*. Murray. 1935.

CONNELL, Brian. *Regina v. Palmerston*. Evans. 1962.

CORTI, Egon. *The English Empress*. Cassell. 1957.

COWLES, Virginia. *Edward VII and His Circle*. Hamish Hamilton. 1956.

CRAWFORD, Emily. *Victoria, Queen and Ruler*. Simpkin, Marshall. 1903.

CRESSWELL, Mrs. G. *Eighteen Years on Sandringham Estate*. Temple Co. 1887.

CRESSWELL, Mrs. G. *Norfolk and the Squires, Clergy, Farmers and Labourers, etc.* Simpkin, Marshall. 1874.

DANGERFIELD, George. *Victoria's Heir.* Constable. 1942.

DENNIS, Geoffrey. *Coronation Commentary.* Dodd, Mead. 1937.

DREW, Mary. *Catherine Gladstone.* Nisbet. 1919.

DUFF, David. *Albert and Victoria.* Muller. 1972.

DUFF, David. *Hessian Tapestry.* Muller. 1967.

DUFF, David. *Victoria Travels.* Muller. 1970.

ESHER, Viscount (Ed.). *The Girlhood of Queen Victoria.* 2 vols. Murray. 1912.

FULFORD, Roger (Ed.). *Dearest Child.* Evans. 1964.

FULFORD, Roger (Ed.). *Dearest Mama.* Evans. 1968.

FULFORD, Roger. *The Prince Consort.* Macmillan. 1949.

GERNSHEIM, H. and A. *Edward VII and Queen Alexandra.* Muller. 1962.

GERSON, N. B. *Lillie Langtry.* Hale. 1972.

GORE, John. *King George V.* Murray. 1941.

GREY, Lt.-Gen. C. *The Early Years of the Prince Consort.* Smith, Elder. 1867.

HARROD, Wilhelmine, and LINNELL, C. L. S. *Norfolk.* Faber & Faber. 1957.

HIBBERT, Christopher. *George IV: Prince of Wales.* Longman. 1972.

HIBBERT, Christopher. *Edward: The Uncrowned King.* Macdonald. 1972.

HOLMES, Sir Richard. *Edward VII.* 2 vols. Amalgamated Press. 1910.

JAGOW, Dr Kurt (Ed.). *Letters of the Prince Consort.* Murray. 1938.

JERROLD, Clare. *The Married Life of Queen Victoria.* Nash. 1913.

JONES, Mrs Herbert. *Sandringham—Past and Present.* Jarrold. 1888.

"J. P. J." *Reminiscences.* Private. 1929.

LEE, Sir Sidney. *King Edward VII.* 2 vols. Macmillan. 1925–7.

LEE, Sidney. *Queen Victoria.* Smith, Elder. 1902.

LONGFORD, Elizabeth. *Victoria R.I.* Weidenfeld & Nicholson. 1964.

MADOL, Hans R. *Christian IX.* Collins. 1939.

MADOL, Hans R. *The Private Life of Queen Alexandra.* Hutchinson. 1940.

MAGNUS, Sir Philip. *King Edward the Seventh.* Murray. 1964.

MARCON, Canon W. H. *The Reminiscences of a Norfolk Parson.* 1933.

MARIE LOUISE, Princess. *My Memories of Six Reigns.* Evans. 1956.

MARTIN, R. B. *The Dust of Combat.* Faber & Faber. 1959.

MARTIN, Theodore. *The Life of the Prince Consort.* Smith, Elder. 1877.

MAUROIS, André. *King Edward and His Times.* Cassell. 1933.

MEE, Arthur (Ed.). *Norfolk.* Hodder & Stoughton. 1940.

MORLEY, John. *The Life of William Ewart Gladstone.* 2 vols. Lloyd. 1908.

NICOLSON, Harold. *King George the Fifth.* Constable. 1952.

PAUL, Thomas. *Britain's King and Queen.* Shaw. 1901.

PLOWDEN, Alison. *Danger to Elizabeth.* Macmillan. 1973.

PONSONBY, Arthur. *Henry Ponsonby.* Macmillan. 1942.

PONSONBY, D. A. *The Lost Duchess*. Chapman & Hall. 1958.

POPE-HENNESSY, James. *Queen Mary*. Allen & Unwin. 1959.

RADNOR, Helen, Countess-Dowager of. *From a Great-Grandmother's Armchair*. Marshall Press. 1928.

SANDERSON, Edgar. *King Edward VII*. 5 vols. Gresham. 1910.

SEWELL, J. P. C. (Ed.). *Personal Letters of King Edward VII*. Hutchinson. 1931.

SHEPPARD, Edgar (Ed.). *George Duke of Cambridge*. 2 vols. Longmans Green. 1907.

SHORE, W. T. *The Baccarat Case*. William Hodge, 1932.

ST AUBYN, Giles. *The Royal George*. Constable. 1963.

TAYLER, A. and H. *The Book of the Duffs*. 2 vols. William Brown.

TISDALL, E. E. P. *Unpredictable Queen*. Stanley Paul. 1953.

TRENCH, C. Chenevix. *George II*. Allen Lane. 1973.

TROWBRIDGE, W. R. H. *Queen Alexandra*. Fisher Unwin. 1921.

VICTORIA, Queen. *More Leaves from the Journal of a Life in the Highlands*. Smith, Elder. 1884.

WATSON, Alfred E. T. *King Edward VII as a Sportsman*. Longmans Green. 1911.

WATSON, Vera. *A Queen at Home*. W. H. Allen. 1952.

WILLIAMS, Neville. *Life and Times of Elizabeth I*. Weidenfeld & Nicolson. 1972.

WINDSOR, Duke of. *A Family Album*. Cassell. 1960.

WINDSOR, Duke of. *A King's Story*. Cassell. 1951.

WORTHAM, H. E. *The Delightful Profession*. Cape. 1931.

WYNDHAM, Mrs. H. (Ed.). *Correspondence of Lady Lyttelton*. Murray. 1912.

Index